Advanced Praise

"*Roost* is nothing less than a handbook for successful chicken keeping nested within Ms. Mitchell-Strong's entertaining and revealing personal narrative. Readers with chickens will immediately recognize themselves in its pages, nodding their heads knowingly as she experiences both the heartbreak and joy that are the chicken keeper's rights of passage."

— Robert Litt, author of *A Chicken in Every Yard: The Urban Farm Store's Guide to Chicken Keeping*

Roost

Roost

Confessions of a First-Time Chicken Farmer

Bronwyn Mitchell-Strong

Apprentice
House Press
Loyola University Maryland

First Edition

Caseboiund ISBN: 978-1-62720-195-7
Paperback ISBN: 978-1-62720-183-4
E-book ISBN: 978-1-62720-184-1

Printed in the United States of America

Interior design by Julia McRae
Cover design by Olivia Airhart & Julia McRae
Marketing by Olivia Airhart
Development by Charlotte Schreyer

Published by Apprentice House

Apprentice House Press
Loyola University Maryland

Apprentice House
Loyola University Maryland
4501 N. Charles Street
Baltimore, MD 21210
410.617.5265 • 410.617.2198 (fax)
www.apprenticehouse.com
info@apprenticehouse.com

Dedicated to the ruler of my roost – Christina

Contents

"People who count their chickens before they are hatched, act very wisely, because chickens run about so absurdly that it is impossible to count them accurately."
— *Oscar Wilde*

Disclaimer

This book should not be taken as a guide to keeping backyard chickens. While there are scientifically based books and authoritative guides on how to raise chickens available online through websites like Backyardchicken.com or Mypetchicken.com, or from your local library, this is not one of them.

Warnings

If you are a farmer, or you grew up on a farm around chickens, do not read this book. It will probably validate your notions that the non-farming community is soft, squeamish, hypocritical, and uninformed. It may also change these notions. Be forewarned.

If you are not a farmer, which is likely the case since 99% of the U.S. population is non-farming, look out, as you are about to acquire an appreciation for the work that farmers do to keep our supermarket shelves stocked and our bellies full – they are the true 1%.

If you are thinking about becoming a backyard chicken farmer and read this book, beware, as this book could very well tip the scales in favor of you taking the plunge. Just know that life is better with chickens.

If you are already a backyard chicken farmer reading this book, you will either see a bit of yourself in these pages and laugh, sit in judgement and laugh, or laugh first, learn from our mistakes, and become better chicken farmers than we.

And if you suffer from Alektorophobia- put this book down immediately, walk away and call your therapist.

An Idea is Hatched

There are many ways to test a new relationship. You can go on a trip together. You can meet the in-laws. You can move in together. You can go shopping at IKEA. Or, if you are like Chris and me, you can get a flock of chickens.

We were a new couple – counting in months rather than years. It was the dead of winter. Snow blanketed the ground. Neither one of us wanted to get out of bed. Chris was dreamily flipping through seed catalogs planning her spring garden while I fell blissfully into and out of sleep.

I'm not sure if I dreamed about chickens, or Chris said something about chickens. Maybe it was divine intervention. For whatever reason, an innocuous enough Google search on the laptop for backyard chickens changed the trajectory of our lives forever.

Once we decided to get chickens, we needed to settle on the size of the flock. Chickens are flock animals. You can't get just one chicken. Being newbies, we decided to go conservative with a starter flock of four.

Which type or types of chickens to get was our next challenge. Just like people, chickens come in all sorts of flavors. There are over 500 different breeds of chickens worldwide. It is important to choose chicken varieties that match the climate you live in as well as your personality. Lucky for us, MyPetChicken.com has a matching app designed to bring the right humans together with the right chickens – "Chicken Tinder?"

Living in the Mid-Atlantic region of the country, we needed chickens that could tolerate searing heat as well as frigid cold.

Happy disposition was also a must. When Chris learned that some chickens lay multi-colored eggs in hues of green and blue, egg color was factored into the algorithm. Based on our geography and personal preferences, we picked two varieties to comprise our flock – Speckled Sussex and Easter Eggers. Based on these descriptions from the website, who could blame us?

Sussex

The Sussex have everything: they are great layers of tinted or light brown eggs--and they lay right through the coldest weather. They are dual purpose birds, though: fat-bodied and not prone to flying when mature, so they are easily fenced. In England, they used to be THE standard table bird, before the modern Cornish Crosses came along. They forage well and are economical eaters that are friendly and easily handled. Their curious nature means they will often follow you around the yard if they think they can beg a treat from you. The "speckled" variety has plumage that gives them some camouflage from predators, too. Many tend to get more speckles after each successive molt, so they just get prettier with age. Seriously, what more could you ask for in a chicken?

Easter Eggers

Easter Eggers are not a breed per se, but a variety of chicken that does not conform to any breed standard but lays large to extra large eggs that vary in shade from blue to green to olive to aqua and sometimes even pinkish. Easter Eggers vary widely in color and conformation, and are exceptionally friendly and hardy. Since they are usually quite friendly to children and humans in general, they are a great choice for a family flock. Most hatcheries mistakenly label their Easter Eggers as Ameraucanas or Araucanas (or various misspellings thereof). True Ameraucanas and Araucanas are currently only available through breeders. Easter Eggers do not qualify to be shown, since they do not conform to a breed standard.

Placing our order in winter with a spring arrival date gave us enough time (or so we thought) to learn everything we needed to and get all the necessary supplies, including a coop.

If settling on breeds of chickens seemed daunting, that was nothing compared to selecting a coop. There must surely be more styles, designs, and pricing options in chicken housing than in people housing. The wide spectrum of coop kits ranges from replicas of Victorian houses to simple box structures. If you're a do-it-yourselfer, there are many examples of creative repurposing of existing or found items into chicken coops; everything from an abandoned Volkswagen Bug to a trampoline. Whether a mansion or a shack, the most important aspect of any coop is its security, for there is no shortage of chicken predators.

Ironically, chicken wire is not a recommended barrier. The openings are too large. An industrious raccoon (and aren't they all industrious?) can easily reach through the wire, grab a chicken by its head and pull. They can also use their teeth to tear through portions of the fencing. Hardware wire mesh is the preferred material which should be used on all sides including the bottom.

With security front of mind, we shopped for a coop. In the end, we opted for a rather simple kit. The bottom floor was a run giving the chickens space to stretch their legs and flap their wings. A ramp led up to an upper chamber that functioned as a nesting and laying area.

Once the chickens and the coop were ordered, supplies and food purchased, it was time to get to work learning all we could about chickens so as to be fully prepared for their arrival.

Baby chicks hatch using an egg tooth to break their way out of their eggshell homes. The tooth drops off after a couple of days. They are shipped from the hatchery the day after they are born. Inside their bellies is enough residual food to last the one-day trip to their new homes. Hand warmers are packed inside the box to keep them warm. The post office calls when the birds arrive.

When our call came, heart racing, I jumped into my car and

headed to the post office. A smile crept across my face at the sound of the chirping peeps coming from the box being held near the counter. Others in line were curious about the sounds and surprised when I explained that I was picking up baby chickens.

They registered a few ounces on the scale, but the weight of the responsibility we were undertaking when I accepted the box from the post office, was almost too heavy to bear. But then I heard the cheeps and chirps of the newest members of our family, and knew right then and there, that no matter what, things were going to be ok.

I had texted Chris when I received the call, and she was waiting at home when I arrived. Together we carefully opened the box, and took a look inside. Thankfully, all four birds were safe and sound. Many suggest that you order one or two more birds than you think you want just in case there is a problem during transport or in the first days of life.

Even after all the hours of study we had done, nothing really prepares you for the reality of becoming a chickeneer. We were more than a wee bit timid and nervous to even pick the chicks up – scared we might hurt them. But we didn't have the luxury of being scared. It was important to get the stressed baby chicks settled in to their new home, warmed up, fed and watered. They had been through a lot in just their first two days of life.

Our makeshift brooder (chicken nursery) was a wired dog crate. A heat lamp was clipped to the crate's roof to keep the temperature at the required 90 degrees. All four chicks took to the crate immediately. They found their food and began eating. They found their water and began drinking. Everything was in order and the initial rush of adrenaline subsided in both of us. We took up two chairs and quietly sat and watched the commencement of our new life with chickens.

Outlaws

Chickens have long played an integral part in human existence. In the olden days, having a few birds at home was the norm, not the exception. That is why in older cities, ordinances on the books today allow for the ownership of chickens. Unfortunately, Chris and I live in the new America: suburbia. With roots that stretch only as far back as the 1950's, suburban laws mirror modern lifestyles – ones that include supermarkets.

Whereas it is legal in most suburbs to own cats, dogs, parrots, ferrets, snakes, and even tigers, keeping chickens is often illegal as it is where we live in the Maryland suburbs. But just ten miles down the road in the City of Baltimore, families are allowed to own chickens (as long as the chickens are 25 ft. away from neighboring property lines). In Baltimore County, however, chickens are only allowed on properties that measure one acre or more. Where chickens are outlawed, only outlaws have chickens. That makes me and Chris outlaws and the chickens illegal aliens.

We entered into this life of crime intentionally and we are not alone. Throughout Maryland and the nation, people are pushing the powers that be to change the laws. Non-violent acts of protest are a hallmark of democracy, and it feels good to be moving the arc of moral judgement, a beak's length closer to justice.

The facts are clear. Chickens pose less of a threat to human welfare and safety than the domestic dog. Backyard chickens provide eggs that are lower in cholesterol and higher in nutritional content than their mass-produced supermarket cousins. The Constitution of the United States grants us the right to life, liberty and the pursuit of happiness. Chickens help sustain life, liberate our food budget, and provide happiness. Is it not therefore, our constitutional right to own chickens? Supreme Court be prepared. The chicken owners of America may be heading your way.

A Chicken By Any Other Name

Typically, farmers don't name their animals. Life and death, food and famine - the circle of life is in constant rotation at a farm. Not being typical farmers, we named our chickens. Choosing a name is sacred business. We could have gone in any number of directions. Three weeks into life with chickens, we opted for sentimentality and decided to name each of the chickens after dear friends of ours: Todd, Nicole, Glynn Ann and Ellen. The namesakes were informed of this great honor via email:

Dear Todd, Nicole, Glynn Ann and Ellen,

Chris and I are lucky to have such a strong network of friends. While strong, that network stretches many thousands of miles. Since meeting for happy hour, brunch, a game of dominoes/backgammon takes planning and plane tickets – Chris and I resorted to the next best thing. By giving each chicken one of your names, we get to have you with us on a daily basis – albeit in a different form. Every time we look at the chickens, we will think of you.

Just like you – each chicken has a distinct look and a distinct personality that continues to evolve daily.

Todd is the blonde chick. She is the most developed in terms of fluff to feather ratio. She is also the bravest when it comes to excursions out of the pen. Todd is the only one of the four that flies up to, and perches on our hands, legs, or shoulders. She does have active bowels which are often voided on those said hands, legs, and shoulders. Todd has a voracious appetite – quick reflexes – and a weird way of eating which involves kicking food out of the container onto the floor for consumption.

Ellen, whose coloration closely resembles that of a hawk, is second behind Todd in terms of development. This makes sense - since both are Easter Eggers. Nicole, however, is fast on her heels. Glynn Ann is the runt of the litter.

Ellen thinks she is the head hen. Todd seemingly ignores Ellen's bitchiness – and Nicole gives as good as she gets. Despite her aggressive ways, Ellen has been slow to perch either on the poles located inside the cage or on the outstretched hands we proffer at each meeting. Nicole is getting braver in that respect – which I think is pissing off Ellen.

Nicole's most striking feature is her eyes. She has very dramatic black streaks that sweep across each eye along the length of her head. She and Glynn Ann look very similar and for a while they were both the same size, however, during the course of her short life, Nicole has turned her back on Glynn Ann, choosing instead to hang out with the "cool crowd" of Todd and Ellen.

Nicole is showing more courage when it comes to exploring outside the cage – and recently attempted to fly into my hand. I wasn't expecting the flight – and was therefore not prepared. Instead of making it into my hand, she plopped a foot in front of me – no harm.

Last – but not least – at least in our eyes is Glynn Anne. She is the smallest of the four – lagging behind in bulk and feathers. Glynn Ann's reflexes are good when it comes to eating bugs. We know this because Chris and I have now taken to collecting doodle bugs (rolly pollies) especially for her and feeding her from our hand. She picks off those bugs like popcorn.

In the cage, however, she is no match for her bigger and more brutish sisters. Whether out of fear or daintiness – Glynn Ann stays on the sideline unwilling to fight over food. She is less lively than the others and tends to like to sleep and stay under the warmth of the heat lamp rather than frolic around scratching the pine shavings or pecking at random items of interest. She surprised us the other day by joining the other three on a short walk about outside of the cage – of her own accord. She is a tender soul – one which Chris and I are taking care to nourish and protect.

The transition from peep to adult chicken is happening rapidly. Changes to their physical selves happen on a daily if not hourly basis. Right now they are all going through a very awkward stage of appearance as the fluff is replaced by feathers.

While they aren't scheduled to start providing eggs for another 6 months, just like you – they provide us with an amazing amount of joy and entertainment. It has taken some time to learn how to properly cuddle with a chicken. There are no big floppy ears or soft bellies to rub. Once the squawking and wing fluttering ceases, we place their legs on our hands or thighs for support and gently rub their backs and chests. It appears that long gentle stroking of the chest is preferred. They are getting used to human contact – though every time we reach for them, it seems to be a very traumatic affair.

We hope that you are honored and touched for the naming was done from a place of love and affection for you all. Calling out their names each day is like having you with us. Thank you for being such integral pieces of our lives. May the flock be with you…

Love – Bronwyn and Christina

Poop – There it is

Chickens like to perch. In the cage, there were two perching poles placed at varying heights. As the chickens developed confidence in their jumping and flying, they spent more and more time above the ground. Todd learned the hard way about gravity. One day when she was on the ground eating and Nicole was resting peacefully on a perch above, nature called Nicole and the contents of her bowels and kidneys (chickens poop and pee in one fell swoop – very efficient) emptied upon the unsuspecting Todd below.

While Todd didn't seem to mind, I did, so I learned via Google how to bathe a chicken. This skill came in handy because as the chicks continued to develop, hygiene or the lack thereof, became more of an issue. As they grew bigger they ate more which meant they pooped more and even more indiscriminately with the ratio of poop to body mass beginning to favor poop.

To be a successful chicken farmer, you have to make peace with the poop. Inside the pen, the poop was absorbed by the inch layer of pine shavings covering the floor. That would be fine if we kept the girls inside the cage at all times. We didn't. Instead, we liked to give them free range of the three-season room, a glassed-in room attached to the side of the house. As such, the floor, carpet, welcome mat, and chairs all fell victim. We fell victim as well, until we learned to identify pre-pooping signs, and adjust our proximity to the chicks' tail feathers accordingly.

We anxiously awaited the day when the chickens would be old enough to move outside to the coop. A case of bleach sat at the ready to sanitize the three-season room. Until then, the poop continued to come.

Spring Chickens

Once the temperatures became temperate enough, Chris and I decided to introduce the flock to the great out of doors. We set up a large pen, and covered it with a tarp to prohibit an aerial escape. One by one, we transported each of the four chicks from the indoor pen outside. It was the first time the chicks' feet had touched grass.

At first, they were a bit confused and scared. They stood around looking at each other – waiting. Todd broke the standstill and began exploring, scratching the earth with her feet and rooting around with her beak. As soon as it became evident that food was underfoot, the others joined in with reckless abandon. The insects, grubs and worms didn't stand a chance against these four, though it seemed that Ellen was maybe a vegetarian as she preferred young clover over insects.

While the pen measured approximately 16 sq. ft. in area, the chicks spent most of the time sticking their heads out through the metal grate walls trying to grab things on the outside. They too must believe that the grass is greener on the other side.

Pecking Order

The chicks were joining a family made up of humans, two cats and a dog. Every day when Chris and I went into the three-season room to spend time with the chickens, the cats – Fluga and Sonny – came along. They stared bright-eyed from the other side of the sliding glass door, watching every flick of every feather.

Sonny was an outdoor cat who enjoys hunting – and not just mice and birds. Sonny once stalked and attacked two deer grazing in the back yard. The deer escaped unharmed, but he did get an unsuspecting rabbit. He was fearless. Though it makes little ecological sense, I wanted to do my best to facilitate an amicable relationship between Sonny and the chicks. Because our family, an often challenging conglomeration of differences and species, should be bound together by love.

So, I began by grabbing the cat, bringing him into the chick room, holding him in my lap, and together we watched the infinitely entertaining exploits of the chickens. At times his body was as stiff as a board and I could feel the adrenaline pulsing through his blood setting his muscles atwitter. At other times, he sat still and feigned indifference. Still when I came in from spending time with the chickens, I made an effort to rub my chicken hands over his face imploring "love the chickens."

Despite our "conditioning" sessions, on the chicks' second venture outside, Sonny struck. My back was to the house, my attention fixed on the chickens and a cold beer. Out of nowhere, an orange flash leaped up and crashed into the metal pen. What Sonny lacked in intelligence was more than made up for by his bravado. Thankfully, I was able to grab him by the scruff of his neck abruptly ending the assault.

It is a delicate ballet we are all performing – Sonny included. The poop laden pine shavings are deposited weekly into the compost pile and later applied to the garden. For breakfast I may eat an egg, provided by family. Dinner may be chicken breast on the grill – a betrayal of family? Mornings, I hunt grubs for the chickens, sustaining the family, and then in the evening pry a chicken from the clutches of a cat, saving the family. The circle of life is spinning madly in the suburbs of Baltimore.

As Happy as a Lark Chicken

The newness of having the chickens soon settled into a simple and efficient routine. Wake up in the morning, head downstairs and let the chickens out of their pen for a walk about in the three-season room. Refill the water and food containers. Toss in some oats and bugs. Chase the chickens back into the pen. Go about the day's business. Return to the pen in the evening. Release the chickens for another walkabout. Check on food and water levels. Return the chickens to the pen. Go to sleep. Wake and repeat.

Subtle changes to the routine were employed in response to the maturation of the chickens. The chickens had learned to remove the top of the food trough and upend the container spilling the entire contents onto the floor of the pen. This in turn compelled the chickens to scratch and sift more than usual thus propelling pine shavings into the water bowl. Both food and water had to be elevated in an attempt to keep the water clean and food stores from being wasted.

Chickens don't wear shoes, but that didn't stop Chris and me from contemplating life on the other side of the pen. On our daily visits, Chris often asked, "Do you think they are happy?" This is a difficult question to answer about any individual let alone one that belongs to another species.

Biologically speaking, the chickens were on target. They had almost insatiable appetites, grew in girth and height, and successfully transitioned from fluff to feather. But were they happy? Their idle chatter peppered the air in pleasing tones. They were ever alert and very active. There was no evident pecking order – no apparent leader. Sure, they occasionally squabbled but what sibling group doesn't?

Still the question of happiness haunted us. To help tilt the happiness scale, Chris and I began to introduce puzzles. A stimulated mind is a happy mind. Instead of simply tossing a handful of clover into the pen – a favorite treat – we placed the clover on top of the cage. In doing so, some of the clover inevitably dropped to the bottom of the pen where it was eagerly feasted upon. However, the true bounty had to first be discovered, then retrieved. We pitted the chickens against the clover in a match of wits reminiscent of Bobby Fisher and Boris Spassky.

Todd was the first to lift his head from the clover that had dropped to the floor to spy the clover overhead. She was visibly intrigued. The earliest adopter of the perching poles, Todd quickly hopped up to one of the two perches positioned across the pen. The clover was so close, she could almost taste it. After a few more tentative steps along the perch, and with an extension of her neck muscles, Todd pecked at the hanging clover.

Instead of landing in her beak, Todd's pecking caused a few more sprigs of clover to dislodge and drop to the floor. Blissfully unaware of Todd, Glynn Ann, Nicole, and Ellen readily accepted this gift from the heavens. Frustrated yet determined, Todd soldiered on. She changed her footing upon the perch and pecked again. This time, she was rewarded with a freshly picked clover flower.

Because birds of a feather flock together, it didn't take long for the three chickens below to begin searching for their missing fourth. In a small pen, measuring but four feet by three feet, the search did not take long. When they stopped eating the magical clover delivered from on high long enough to look up, there they saw Todd sitting on top of the known world busying herself with a clover mother lode.

Ellen quickly deciphered the situation, leaped up and began to peck at the mass. Like Todd's early efforts, Ellen's actions caused more clover to fall. With two fewer chickens now in competition for the fallen clover, Glynn Ann and Nicole stayed on terra firma enjoying gifts from above.

Ellen eventually figured out how to position herself on the perch in a way that allowed her to successfully pluck clover. However, a tipping point is soon reached wherein the stability of the clover bunch is compromised and it cascades to the floor. At this point, Ellen and Todd descended to join Glynn Ann and Nicole in finishing off the lot.

Fledglings

While it was true that at five weeks they were no longer chicks, they also were not considered to be fully matured. At this stage, chickens are classified as immature juveniles. In human terms, they are teenagers. In chickens at this stage as in human teenagers, there is a major disconnect between what they think they know and what they actually know.

Touch is an important component to human happiness. It stood to reason for us, that the same could be true for chickens. Confident that it was in their best interest, Chris and I made a habit of physically handling the chickens on a daily basis whether they liked it or not. Like their human teenager counterparts, the chickens met these displays of affection with squawks and feather ruffling. We hoped that also like their teenaged counterparts, the protest was merely a front concealing their true feelings of love.

Empty Nesters

At seven weeks, the chickens were physically ready. Chris and I were emotionally ready. It was time to transition the chickens from their indoor brooding facility to an outdoor coop.

Fully constructed, the Cape Cod style coop is five feet by three feet and stands four feet high. It has an open-air design bound on all sides with either heavy gauge wire mesh or wood paneling. There is a loft-style enclosed bedding area which opens into a two-chamber laying station. A handle affixed to the door, allows us to shut the hens in for the night and release them in the morning. The bedding chamber, while enclosed, has an exterior door with a four-paned glass window. This allows for additional access to the chickens and provides ambient lighting which is important in regulating the sleeping patterns of diurnal animals.

Ingress and egress to the loft is made via a wooden ramp covered in a no-slip surface. The bottom of the coop is fully meshed to prevent predatory entry. Access to the laying chamber – and ultimately the eggs (fingers crossed) is made through an external hatch that functions as the roof to the chamber. The wood is non-rotting cedar that has been stained an attractive shade of mahogany. The unit is both attractive and practical. According to the description, this particular coop is sized to house up to six full-grown chickens.

Because the description stated that the coop was large enough for six chickens, we naturally reasoned that it would be downright spacious for a flock of four. However, as we gazed proudly upon the completed coop, Chris and I both wondered whether it would be large enough to comfortably house the four chickens.

Call it coop envy, buyer's remorse, or anthropomorphizing, we chicken novices believed that the chickens would need more space than this coop provided. These were American suburban chickens. If the houses and cars were oversized, so too should be the coop.

Our first thought was to build an extension to the existing coop structure. Many a martini was consumed while standing around the coop hatching ways to construct a viable addition. In the end, the design that won out was not an addition at all, but a second stand-alone structure. Positioned close enough to the coop to easily facilitate transfer from one structure to another, this secondary coop would be self-contained. Less secure than the main coop, coop deux would be used only during the day and only with an adult presence.

In time, Chris and I hoped to allow the chickens to free range a portion of the day under our supervision. However, because these are illegal outlaw chickens, we lived in constant fear of their deportation. This secondary pen would provide the space we felt the chickens needed for a high quality of life while allowing them to fly below the radar of nosey neighboring eyes.

When trying to build an extension to a coop that already cost $400 dollars or approximately 133 dozen eggs, frugality trumped the experts. The recommended galvanized wire mesh, while strong, durable and predator proof, is pricey. After weighing all of the options, Chris and I purchased 50 feet of rabbit wire and 25 feet of aluminum screen along with timber for a frame. The structure would be strong and durable yet not fully predator proof. Since this was for day use only, we compromised on the security knowing that when the night lurking predators come a calling, the chickens will be safe and secure in the main coop.

We had a three-season room full of poop, a fully constructed coop and annex, and balmy ambient temperatures. We spread a liberal layer of clean pine shavings on the floor of the coop and inside the sleeping and laying chambers. It was time to introduce the chickens to their new home.

I knelt down on the poop laden floor of the three-season room and one by one, grabbed Todd, Nicole, Glynn Ann and Ellen and handed them to Chris. As the cool morning air of the outdoors hit each of their beaks, they stopped struggling and stopped squawking. Their calm exteriors bellied a sense of excitement and anticipation which was felt communally in both chicken and human.

All four of the chickens were carefully placed on the floor of the pen along with the ritual morning handful of clover. For a moment the chickens stood still trying to comprehend how in five minutes, their lives could have changed so dramatically. Unable to do so, they simply began to eat the clover and explore.

Life inside the coop was carefree. There was a lot of food and no predators. Outside of the coop, reward is balanced by risk. In a world where everything tastes like chicken, no chicken is safe – not even in the suburbs of Baltimore. Birds of prey like hawks and owls, raccoons, weasels, foxes, snakes and domesticated cats would kill for a chicken dinner.

Unlike the dog crate/brooder, the coop has a separate room for sleeping and the laying of eggs. There is a door to this room that can be left open to provide free movement, or locked shut. On this first day after the big move and not knowing any better, I reasoned that as human protector, it was my responsibility to lock the chickens up for the night.

When they saw me coming, they perked up anxiously awaiting the handful of treats that accompanies my visits. This time there were no treats. Instead I carefully unlatched the main door to the coop and began picking chickens up and putting them in the sleeping chamber. It wasn't the easiest of things to do, but eventually, all four chickens were safely locked in the sleeping chamber. As I retired for the evening to my own sleeping chamber, I glanced back at the coop and could just make out Glynn Ann pecking furiously at the window in Morse Code pleading to be let out.

The next morning, I went down to the coop and peaked in the window to the sleeping chamber. The chickens were awake and waiting for me. I pulled the door to the sleeping chamber open, and one by one, the chickens filed down the ramp into the coop, pausing briefly to stretch a leg before diving into the handful of fresh clover.

The chickens were adjusting and seemed content, if not downright happy with their new abode. Day two quickly turned into night two which led me to my first chicken crossroads. While I genuinely cared for the chickens, the thought of putting them to bed with the same frustrations of the night before, night in and night out for the next six years (the average laying time for a chicken) had me thinking chicken dinner.

Luckily, my worry was in vain. As I approached the coop that second night, it was empty. Without provocation or fuss, all four chickens had retreated to the sleeping chamber. As quietly as I could, I shut the door and said good night to the four happiest, smartest, and most well-adjusted chickens in the world.

Chicken Crack

An empty nest isn't all that it's cracked up to be. Chris and I had anxiously counted the days until the girls were old enough to move out of the house and into the coop. There were no tears on moving day. The chickens settled right in, and Chris and I reclaimed the three-season porch. With every transition however, there are challenges. The chickens adjusted just fine. It took the humans a bit longer.

Having the chickens indoors had its advantages. The confined space allowed no room for escape, provided us with the advantage when it was time to round everyone up for the night, and made it easy to care and tend for them in all weather conditions. Inside, the humans were fully in control. Outside, the balance of power shifted in favor of the chickens.

As outlaw chickens, Nicole, Glynn Ann, Ellen and Todd were forced to live in the shadows. However, happy chickens need space to scratch, peck, and spread their wings. The annex, a 48-sq. ft. pen, was constructed to give the chickens room to roam yet remain sheltered and secure. Summer foliage around the property helped to conceal their existence from neighbors.

Transferring chickens from coop to annex became number two on the morning to do list just after going number one and before coffee. In pajamas, and flip-flops, one or the other of us would walk across the house, open the back door, greet the day and greet the chickens. The chickens had come to recognize the sound of the backdoor. They all huddle next to the door of the coop vocalizing their excitement.

The annex was originally built as a fixed structure, its support frame tied to the earth. It was positioned near enough to the coop so that the entrance to the annex corresponded to the door to the coop. The design allowed for easy ingress and egress from the coop to the annex and vice versa. In the morning, the doors were opened, and the chickens enthusiastically ran, hopped, or flew into the annex. In the evening, the chickens, always eager to sink their beaks into fresh clover, happily ran back into the coop as clover was tossed inside.

Two weeks into this routine, Chris and I realized a design flaw. Our happy chickens had pecked, scratched, and pooped their way through every single blade of grass within the annex leaving nothing but bare soil. It wasn't the loss of lawn that was the problem. It was the denuded living space. Like humans, chickens enjoy stimulation. Without grass and grubs, we figured the chickens would become bored and depressed. Therefore, to keep the chickens happy, the fixed structure would need to be reconfigured into a mobile unit ensuring a fresh supply of insects and greenery.

While this arrangement made for happy chickens and a greener lawn, it created a new challenge. With the annex located away from the coop, the only way to ensure safe transport to and from the annex was to tuck a chicken under an arm.

Each time we entered the coop, the chickens squawked furiously at the intrusion. Though barely a pound each in size, chickens are unnaturally strong. We learned early on that there can be no timidity when attempting to capture a chicken.

Ellen and Todd were the most difficult to handle. They squawked the loudest, flapped their wings, and flew around the coop to avoid capture. Nicole and Glynn Ann seemed to better understand that the intrusion into their personal space was a necessary temporary inconvenience, and managed to suffer the indignation in silence.

As a reward, once the chickens were safely ensconced in the annex, bunches of clover were shoved into the wire frame. At the first sight of clover, all was forgiven.

In the evening, the chickens had to be transported from the annex back into the coop. This was infinitely more challenging than moving them from the coop into the annex. First, the top of the annex was removed allowing one to fully enter the enclosure. Chickens can and do fly. With the top off, they could easily fly out of the annex and into the yard. Though smarter than your average chickens, their brains were still the size of the fingernail on a small finger, and for a full month they simply ran around the coop trying to escape capture rather than taking to the air. Advantage human.

However, running around the annex trying to round up four chickens makes herding cats seem like child's play. After a month of chasing chickens, the desire for eggs was being slowly eclipsed with the thought of chicken soup. Then it happened.

The chickens, it seemed, had also had enough of this evening ritual and one by one, with Todd in the lead, they broke free from the annex. Todd hopped over the wall and Ellen and Nicole broke through the door that I forgot to latch upon entering the annex. Chris and I had planned on eventually letting the chickens roam freely in the yard, under close supervision. That day had evidently arrived.

Three of the four chickens were out while Glynn Ann was tucked under my arm. Recognizing the futility of the situation, I released Glynn Ann to join the others.

Free to roam, the chickens stayed close together and close to the house. The chickens reveled in the new environment. I was terrified. Without any type of enclosure, how in the hell would I be able to capture or coax the chickens back into the coop. Any attempt to get close to a chicken resulted in the chicken running in the opposite direction. They were no fools.

Chris tried the Jurassic Park method. In the movie, the dinosaurs couldn't see a human unless they moved. Because of the evolutionary connection between dinosaurs and birds, Chris thought if she stood still, and let the chickens come to her, she would be able to swoop down and scoop one up like a Tyrannosaurus Rex. Again, the chickens' reflexes proved far superior.

Then I remembered, yogurt. During our pre-chicken research phase, Chris and I visited with a friend who is also raising outlaw chickens in the suburbs. As night began to fall and her chickens were out and about free ranging, instead of running feverishly around the yard trying to herd the chickens home, she instructed her daughter to go get the yogurt. She told us that her chickens loved yogurt.

With this nugget of information retrieved from my brain's file cabinet, Chris went inside to get some yogurt. I held the container out to the chickens. At first, they moved away. I stayed stationary holding the container down at beak level. Nicole expressed some interest and began to timidly approach. I froze every muscle in my body not wanting to make any sort of movement that would cause Nicole to flee. Suddenly, Nicole stuck her beak into the yogurt, swallowed, and repeated.

When one chicken finds something good to eat, they all want in on it. A large insect that finds its way into one chicken's beak will often find its way into another chicken's stomach because they fight over the good stuff. Yogurt is the good stuff.

As soon as the others noticed Nicole indulging in the yogurt, they all came to investigate. After one bite they were hooked. Never before had I seen the birds so ferociously attack anything that was not an insect   not clover, nothing. The yogurt that remained on the outside of a beak was quickly eaten off by one of the other chickens.

Slowly, I walked backwards holding the container down where they could see it and remarkably, they followed. I stopped, let them peck a bit more at the yogurt and then took a few more steps backwards. This process was repeated until I made it to the door of the coop. Here came the real test. I gently placed the container into the coop and stepped away. They could have easily turned around and headed back for the bushes, but the draw from the yogurt was too strong. They were powerless against it. In they went, one by one. No squawks, no ruffled feathers. I closed the door to the coop behind them. They didn't even notice. All four heads were fully immersed in yogurt.

Based on that success, Chris and I decided to test the yogurt again the next evening. This time we purposefully let all four chickens out of the annex for some well-deserved yet supervised "wild time." After about an hour, it was time for the yogurt. Placed in the same container, I held out the yogurt for the chickens. This time, Nicole came almost immediately with the others close behind. Slowly, yet more quickly than the day before, I walked backwards towards the coop. The chickens followed. I placed the container on the floor of the coop, stepped away, and just like before, all four chickens walked right into the coop interested only in the yogurt.

Unless chickens have developed some weird heretofore unknown relationship with cows (who knows what goes on down on the farm when the humans aren't watching), yogurt bears no relation to anything chickens would consume in the wild. This makes their affinity to yogurt so perplexing. But there is an affinity. An affinity so strong it overrides the flight or fight mechanism in their brains. It is chicken crack. We buy it in bulk.

The yogurt discovery had once again tilted the balance of power into our favor, and resulted in a win-win situation for all. The chickens got to enjoy daily "wild time" outside of the annex and the coop. Chris and I got to enjoy an afternoon cocktail with the chickens while supervising their explorations instead of spending half an hour chasing the chickens.

If the current trend in backyard chicken farming continues to rise, a good investment may be yogurt stocks.

Don't Count Your Eggs Before They Are Laid

Forget about a watched pot. A watched hen seemingly never lays. "The Girls" had just celebrated their 4-month birthdays when Chris and I broke down and purchased a dozen eggs at the grocery store. We hemmed and hawed, said yes then no before settling finally on yes. Of course, all of the chicken websites told us not to expect eggs until at least 20 weeks. For the varieties we have Speckled Sussex and Easter Eggers   even 20 weeks is optimistic. In reality we were looking at five to six months before laying commenced. It was unreasonable to expect eggs any sooner, but then again, our chickens were smarter and more mature than the average chicken.

So sure of my chickens, I wagered that the first egg would be laid on August 17 – a mere three and a half months into their earthly existence. Unlike the chickens, I was keenly aware of the date, and paid close attention to their actions on that particular day. They did not disappoint.

Nearing dusk, I noticed some strange behavior. I saw Todd and Ellen lying on the ground, their beaks ferociously pecking the grass to expose soil. The chickens, up until that point had never rested from scratching and pecking to retrieve food. This was something entirely different. Sensing a historic moment, I grabbed my phone, a beer and a chair, and headed out to the annex to catch the first egg on film.

The peculiar behavior continued. There in the middle of the annex was a patch of bare soil where once there was grass. Todd and Ellen continued to peck at the ground, seemingly eating dirt, and creating a cavity in the ground. To my untrained eye, they were creating a nest into which an egg would soon be deposited.

So engaged in their engineering, neither Todd nor Ellen took notice of my position just outside the annex wall. The digging continued unabated. Nicole and Glynn Ann, the two Speckled Sussex, were only mildly interested. Every once in a while, they would check in on the progress of the other two, but they mainly contented themselves with a discarded watermelon rind.

As Todd and Ellen's behavior became more and more peculiar, I became more excited and began to film. The two chickens flapped their wings and rolled around the ground on their sides and backs. If I had an egg in me that I wanted to get out, I too would be rolling around on the ground. I figured things were definitely progressing in the right direction.

I filmed in two-minute stints, waited a few minutes and began filming again. Jane Goodall of chimpanzee fame indicated that her passion for natural history was first sparked as a small child when, determined to learn how an egg is produced by a chicken, hid in a coop for four hours waiting for a chicken to come and lay while her parents searched for her, calling the police, thinking the worst. Having witnessed the egg appear and drop from the chicken into the soft hay below, Jane ran home to share her findings with her mom, who, instead of scolding, sat and listened thoughtfully about Jane's amazing discovery.

Thoughts of young Jane passed through my mind as I sat stone still watching Todd and Ellen roll around in the dirt. What Jane didn't have was a handheld video camera in a phone with one button upload to YouTube. In addition to young Jane, my mind was also counting millions of viewer hits.

A full hour passed. My phone's video limit had been reached, but still no egg. Just before running inside to grab another beer, Todd and Ellen bounced up, shook their feathers loose of dirt, and joined Nicole and Glynn Ann at the watermelon rind.

Not ready to admit defeat, I rationalized that this was a trial run and eggs were definitely on the near-frame horizon. I was wrong.

What I had witnessed was a simple case of chicken grooming – the dirt bath.

The next day, and most days following, all four chickens engaged in the same ritual. However instead of the annex, they christened a patch of loose soil beneath a boxwood bush as the official bath site.

They pecked and scratched out personal divots in the earth and proceeded to kick soil into their feathers. No feather was immune. Each was doused with as much soil as was available. Todd, being pure white, underwent a dramatic transformation to black while the others their multi-colored feathers managed to hide the dirt. During the bath, the chickens vocalized in a euphoric chirping sound that best resembles a cat purring. They entered an ecstatic trance which made it very easy for them to be scooped up and deposited into the coop for the night. So much dirt was deposited into the feather folds that it doubled the weight of each bird.

On average, the bathing ritual lasted anywhere from 30 minutes to an hour giving Chris and I the opportunity to engage in our nightly ritual – the cocktail. This seems quite apropos as the word cocktail is said to have originated in New Orleans where an apothecary by the name of Peychaud (of bitters fame) served a mixed brandy drink in a French eggcup – referred to as a coquetier. The word was shortened first to "cocktay" and ultimately to "cocktail."

According to MyPetChicken.com, dust baths are absolutely necessary for chickens. They prevent parasites such as mites and lice from finding a home in your chickens' feathers and legs.

Therefore, what I witnessed was a rite of passage, just not the one that I had hoped for. It was safe to report that the chickens were mite, lice, and unfortunately still egg free. Luckily time marches on.

To help inspire the chickens to lay, Chris and I, on advice from our fellow suburban chicken farmer and our chicken mentor, Coreen, deposited four golf balls into their sphere of reference. Two were placed in the coop and two in the annex. Apparently if there are no egg-laying chickens about, the golf balls work to stimulate egg laying. Once the golf balls were introduced to Coreen's flock, it took only four days before her chickens began to lay. After 10 days of the balls being in play at our "farm," still no eggs. Instead of stimulating the chickens, the balls, especially when viewed first thing in the morning prior to a cup of coffee, elicited an outflow of adrenaline in the humans who, knowing better, continued to mistake the balls for eggs.

Great Eggspectations

Ellen was acting a bit strange before Chris and I departed for Chicago to cheer on human Todd and Nicole in their annual marathon tradition. Unless one of us was holding in our hand a bowl of yogurt, the chickens, all of them, would usually run, hop or fly away when approached. But the day before we left, Ellen hopped up onto the ledge of the garden positioning herself within my reach. I stretched out my hand, anticipating her turning the other way. Instead she stood there and accepted a series of loving strokes. Though I thought it endearing, I looked upon the incident as an anomaly and mentally filed it away.

Finding people to care for the dog and cats when the humans are away is pretty easy and straight forward. When the plan to raise a flock of chickens was first hatched, Chris and I thought of seemingly everything but care for the flock while on vacation. It is not that looking after the flock is difficult. It is just that chicken care is not a skill set owned by many in the urban/suburban landscape in which we live.

Luckily, friends Anne and David, along with their flock of children and one dog agreed to house sit while we were in Chicago. I wrote out exhaustive notes. Unsure of their capacity to execute the ballet of getting the chickens into and out of the annex, I directed them to keep the birds confined to the coop. That left their only job to make sure the food and water were adequately supplied. As an afterthought, I added that they should check the coop daily for the unlikely arrival of an egg.

Chris and I had each been checking daily for months. Like

high school seniors checking the mailbox for letters of acceptance from the college of their choice, each day we marched out to the coop and opened the hatch to the laying box hoping for an egg. We searched futilely in every nook and cranny, upending the collection of hay and pine shavings, before closing the hatch and returning to the kitchen to announce to the other, dejectedly, no egg.

It was Saturday in Chicago. We had just enjoyed a luxurious brunch at a new upscale sports bar on the bank of Lake Michigan when Chris received a text from Anne stating that we should contact her immediately. Since arriving at our house on Friday night, Anne and David had already called, emailed and texted a handful of times asking for the whereabouts of various spices, pot holders, and extra towels. Therefore, we didn't place much urgency into this particular request.

Anne texted again. This time, attached to the text was a picture of Chloe, Anne's daughter, holding two eggs, one in each hand. One of the eggs was decidedly smaller than the other. The caption noted that the egg on the left was from the refrigerator hinting that the one on the right may have come from some other place. Could it be?

It was hard to tell exactly from the picture, but the egg on the right seemed to have a slight blue color. Chris made the call. According to Anne, the egg was found in the coop sitting next to one of the golf balls we had inserted a month previous in order to stimulate production.

I was both excited and furious. The elusive egg had finally arrived, and we weren't there when it did. To continue the earlier metaphor, it was as if the acceptance letter arrived and the student's parents opened the letter first. The anger and disappointment of not being present for the first egg slowly gave way to pure happiness.

We arrived home Sunday midnight. There it was waiting for

us on the kitchen counter. Like a precious jewel, small, perfect, and glowing pastel blue. The blue color indicated that the egg emanated from one of the two Easter eggers, either Todd or Ellen. Because of that strange behavior pre-departure, I was pretty sure that it was Ellen who had earned the honor. Before going to sleep that night, Chris and I took a flashlight out to the coop and peered inside, hoping to recover egg number two. We found just four sleeping chickens.

The next day, there was a spring in our step as we headed down to the coop. The girls, as per the norm, were up and itching to be let out ready for some much-deserved free range time. After letting them out, we opened the hatch to the laying box, ready to collect the next egg. We were greeted only by piles of chicken poo.

Ellen continued acting differently from the other girls. While Glynn Ann, Todd, and Nicole went out and about in the yard scratching and exploring, Ellen stayed close to the coop and next to us. I bent down towards Ellen and like the day before we left for Chicago, she didn't move. Well, that's not entirely true. As I bent down, she went from a stand to a squat, and then accepted a series of loving strokes to her head and back.

As I walked around the yard preparing the annex and getting the day's supply of food and water, Ellen followed me. Every time I stopped and stooped down towards her, she would assume a squatting position and allow me to pet her. I tried to reach out to the other three. They neither stood still nor squatted. Instead they fretted away and contented themselves with eating.

The squatting behavior is one adopted by laying chickens. It is a sign that hens use to signal to males that they are of laying maturity, and is the submissive position they assume prior to being mounted by a rooster. Where there is no rooster, smaller hens may squat to larger hens or, in our case, to a human as the defacto rooster. It is also a defensive maneuver that camouflages the bird from aerial predators that often hone in on prey through movement. The mystery had been solved. Ellen had indeed laid the first egg.

I kept a close eye on the chickens all day. Except for Ellen's squatting, the day progressed like all the others. The chickens enjoyed the annex, had free range time, but produced no egg. Two more days passed, and still no egg. When laying begins, it is often erratic at first before settling in to a more predictive schedule. Laying frequency is also governed by seasonal changes, weather, and each hen's personal inclinations.

On that Wednesday, five days after the initial egg was discovered, there was second egg, and life was good on the suburban farm.

Walking On Egg Shells

Old sayings age because they are good. "Be careful what you wish for, you might just get it," is a saying that has stood the test of time for good reason. Chris and I had waited for nearly six months for the two eggs that now resided in the basket on the kitchen counter. Fresh eggs, right out of a chicken, have an invisible natural antibacterial membrane called the bloom. This membrane stays in place unless it is washed off. Eggs purchased in a grocery store have had their blooms washed away. That is why they must be stored in a refrigerator.

Fresh "unwashed" eggs can be kept at room temperature for up to a month. You can clean them using a dry cloth or paper towel to remove dirt and debris without disturbing the bloom. If the egg is just too soiled to keep on a counter, it is best to wash it. No detergents are necessary. However, you may wish to employ the help of science. Cold water causes the contents of the egg to shrink. This creates a vacuum that pulls bacteria in through the pores of the shell. Washing with warm water has the opposite effect. NOTE: all eggs should be thoroughly washed with water prior to use.

How does care of homegrown eggs compare with commercially sold eggs? According to USDA regulations, farmers have 30 days to get an egg from the farm to a store. Stores are then given another 30 days to sell the eggs. These days, most, if not all eggs arrive at a store no more than three days after packaging. The USDA recommends five weeks as the maximum time before an egg is used. You can find out how old your eggs are by checking the carton date.

USDA Egg Storage Chart		
Product	**Refrigerator**	**Freezer**
Raw eggs in shell	3 to 5 weeks	Do not freeze.
Raw egg whites	2 to 4 days	12 months
Raw egg yolks	2 to 4 days	Yolks do not freeze well.
Raw egg accidentally frozen in shell	Use immediately after thawing.	Keep frozen; then refrigerate to thaw.
Hard-cooked eggs	1 week	Do not freeze.
Egg substitutes, liquid Unopened	10 days	Do not freeze.
Egg substitutes, liquid Opened	3 days	Do not freeze.
Egg substitutes, frozen Unopened	After thawing, 7 days, or refer to "Use-By" date on carton.	12 months
Egg substitutes, frozen Opened	After thawing, 3 days, or refer to "Use-By" date on carton.	Do not freeze.
Casseroles made with eggs	3 to 4 days	After baking, 2 to 3 months.
Eggnog, commercial	3 to 5 days	6 months
Eggnog, homemade	2 to 4 days	Do not freeze.
Pies, pumpkin or pecan	3 to 4 days	After baking, 1 to 2 months.
Pies, custard and chiffon	3 to 4 days	Do not freeze.
Quiche with any kind of filling	3 to 4 days	After baking, 1 to 2 months.

With our fresh as fresh can be eggs on hand, Chris and I were ready to have our first homegrown breakfast. When cracked open, these eggs had larger yolks that sat up higher and had a richer color of yellowish orange than their commercial counterparts.

Chris and I seemed to linger in the admiration phase of the meal a bit longer than usual. Having a personal relationship with one's food makes the dining experience a more intimate affair. This is both good and a little weird. As we began to eat our $400-dollar eggs, our joy and excitement was tempered by a slight ick factor as our minds grappled with images of chicken butts which thankfully faded with the first bite. The eggs were good, richer in flavor than ordinary store-bought eggs – and healthier too.

According to the USDA, farm fresh eggs have

- 1/3 less cholesterol

- 1/4 less saturated fat

- 2/3 more vitamin A

- 2 times more omega-3 fatty acids

- 3 times more vitamin E

- 7 times more beta carotene.

After some fits and starts, Ellen began to lay regularly, once a day. Forget about everything you have seen on TV or in the movies with the farm boy or girl going out to fetch the eggs at dawn. Our chickens apparently preferred a mid-morning or early afternoon lay.

When Ellen got into a laying mood, she became very agitated and very vocal. She paced the edges of the annex squawking madly. When I saw this change in behavior, I headed out to the annex and opened the door. Ellen would come willingly into my arms and I would transport her to the coop, away from the other girls for some private time. Inside the coop, the pacing continued. She ran up and down the stairway and into and out of the laying box before settling in. Once inside, she constructed a nest, hollowing out a center cavity in the pine shavings just large enough to hold her body and the egg on the way. Once settled in, she quieted down and began to concentrate intently on the task at hand. In all it took an hour or so to complete the process which ended with a quiet thud as the egg dislodged and fell into the nest. At that point, Ellen was up and out of the laying box squawking her desire to rejoin the flock. I was happy to oblige her. I then collected the egg, which was still very warm, and added it to the cute brass egg basket sitting on the kitchen counter.

Is it indulgent to cater to the moods and whims of a chicken? Yes. As the novelty of the egg laying wore off, so too did my desire and inclination to keep moving Ellen from annex to coop and back again to facilitate egg laying. Therefore, I mustered up my nerve and drew a line in the sand. Despite the frantic pacing and squawking, I refused to move Ellen into the coop to lay her egg. It wasn't easy watching from the kitchen window as she expressed signs of distress and panic. But in the end, nature won over nurture and eggs were successfully laid in the annex. The exercise had a two-fold purpose. First, we proved that annex laying was possible. Second was the behavior modeling.

As soon as Ellen started laying, we were sure that the others would follow. Like sorority sisters, or work mates whose menstrual cycles sync up, once one chicken begins to lay, the others are supposed to follow. Yet day after day after day, Ellen remained the only one of the four who assumed the squatting position. And more telling, she was the only one who laid an egg. One egg a day is better than none, but definitely not as good as four.

Despite the successful annex lay, it was obvious that Ellen craved a measure of privacy in which to lay. Perhaps the lack of privacy in the open aired annex was holding the other three back from laying as well. To try to solve the problem, Chris went to work building a three-sided nesting box out of an old table and some discarded shelving and she placed it in the annex. For added encouragement, she stenciled the top of the box with the words "Fresh Eggs Here."

Each day thereafter, we waited and watched. Not only did no other chicken lay an egg, there was no shift in behavior patterns, i.e. no squatting. In fact, it appeared that Nicole, Todd, and Glyn Ann were perfectly happy letting Ellen do all of the heavy lifting.

They seemed oblivious to Ellen's actions and expressed no interest whatsoever in any egg, even when it was laid right in front of them. They also had the gall to use the newly fashioned laying box as a poop depository.

Biologically speaking, they had yet to cross the six-month threshold of life and therefore the upper end of the time to begin laying. Yet I still felt betrayed. Chris and I had poured our heart, soul, sweat, and money into these birds. It was time to realize a real return on the investment.

If Ellen's laying, and the addition of a laying box to the annex were not motivation enough, I had to dig down in my human bag of tricks in order to spur the slackers to action. I chose greed and envy. As the building blocks of capitalism, I believed they held the key to solving our production problems.

Each day after Ellen successfully laid, I would head to the wood pile to dig up a handful of worms and grubs, march over to the annex and hand feed them to her right in full view of the other chickens. The others would try desperately to snatch the worms from my hand as I held them out to Ellen, or try to steal the worms right from her mouth. But we worked out a pretty efficient delivery system ensuring that she was able to consume upwards of 99% of the bounty.

Operation greed continued for another two weeks during which time all four chickens celebrated their 6-month birthday. Still, and much to our dissatisfaction, Ellen was the only one laying, which led me to believe that Nicole, Todd, and Glynn Ann most certainly were "pinko commie" chickens.

Hope began to wane as the clock ticked down to Thanksgiving and what would be our last resort. If there are no atheists in fox holes, then it stands to reason there are no eggless chickens on Thanksgiving. Life is full of difficult choices. I just hoped the girls would make the right choice before it was too late.

Presidential Pardon

In 1989, George H. W. Bush, the 41st President of the United States made history by granting the first "official" presidential pardon to a turkey. The history of presidents and turkeys how-ever, dates as far back as the 19th century. Like country doctors accepting chickens as payment for services, it was commonplace for citizens to gift the president with the finest of their flock. In 1947, the National Turkey Federation became the official turkey supplier to the President. This same year, the official turkey receiv-ing ceremony commenced in the Rose Garden. After their photo with the President, the turkeys' luck ran out as they were summarily incorporated into the Thanksgiving feast. There were, however, the occasional exceptions.

In the 1860's, bowing to the pressure from his son, Tad, who begged his father to grant a pardon to the turkey, President Lincoln let the presidential turkey live. Nearly 100 Thanksgivings later, President Kennedy sent a gifted turkey home. It was during the Nixon Administration when the precedent was set to spare the life of the turkey, sending it to a petting farm near Washington D.C. However, it wasn't until 1989, with animal rights activist picket-ing outside the gates of the White House that the actual president, President H.W. Bush, personally issued the presidential pardon – a tradition that has been adopted by every president since.

Thanksgiving was fast approaching.

Todd had shaken his tailfeathers enough to join Ellen in the ring of glory, but it was literally do or die time for Nicole and Glynn Ann, who despite being given proper care, an abundance of food, and probably an overabundance of human affection, had yet to lay an egg. Chris threw down the gauntlet, stating that come Thanksgiving, any chicken not producing eggs would contribute to the family's dietary needs in a different form. The pressure was on. The clock continued to tick.

I was paying especially close attention to both Nicole and Glynn Ann, hoping to witness the tell-tale sign that laying was imminent, the submissive squat. There was running, hopping, fly-ing, and sitting, but no squat. Each day, I approached the coop with guarded anticipation, hoping to lift the cover and find a brown egg. The only eggs to be had were blue.

I called on the powers of rationalization to counteract the worry regarding the impending deadline. Chris and I were man-aging just fine on the two eggs a day being faithfully produced by Todd and Ellen. We had not only enough to supply our own needs, but we were able to give away eggs to friends and family. A dou-bling of output may in fact be a burden of excess. On the other hand, non-producing chickens still consume feed. Were our flock to decrease in size, so too would our expenses. And then killing and eating an animal builds character and . . .

But I just wasn't ready to give up on my two speckled Sussex. Like Tad, Abraham Lincoln's son, I went to Chris and pleaded for mercy on behalf of Nicole and Glynn Ann. Her mind was made up. She was sticking to her guns. No eggs, no deal.

I scratched around for another angle and found one. We were not hosting Thanksgiving Dinner. This year, we were heading up to Pittsburgh to celebrate the holiday with Chris' family. The menu was already set, with little to no room for changes or additions. And presenting her mother with a freshly butchered chicken would probably not be as well received as a case of red wine, which I vol-unteered to purchase. I could see Chris playing over the scenes in her head. My arguments were gaining momentum. And like Abe

Lincoln appeasing his son, she relented by moving the deadline back four weeks to Christmas.

That evening, I shared the news with Nicole and Glynn Ann. They were nonplussed. It didn't seem to bother them one way or the other. Frustrated at their lack of appreciation, I decided that I would do everything in my power to facilitate the egg laying, short of laying one myself.

I consulted the great chicken oracle, Google, for advice and guidance. There was none. I was on my own, a trailblazer. In movies, to encourage labor in human pregnancies, doctors recommend walking, eating spicy food and engaging in sexual intercourse. The latter two options were clearly not up for consideration as chickens don't taste or recognize food as spicy, and there are some lines that even the most avid of chicken keepers will not cross.

I focused on the walking. If walking was good, maybe running would be better. I proceeded to engage Nicole and Glynn Ann in that most apropos of games, the game of chicken. The chickens apparently didn't understand the game or were confusing it with tag. Instead of running towards each other and waiting to see who veers off course the first, as soon as I made a move towards them, they turned and ran away in the opposite direction. While I would have preferred the game to have been played correctly, the main purpose of the exercise was being realized. The chickens were running round the yard, hopefully spurring on egg-production.

My second strategy involved the element of surprise and fright. I reasoned that if when an animal is scared, including humans, they lose control of their bodily functions and urinate, then maybe the same sort of fright could induce an egg to pop out. If not that, maybe the sudden surge of adrenaline could do the trick. After a few rounds of chicken/tag, the game switched to hide and go seek. Again there was some major confusion regarding the rules of the game. The alternative rules used for the purpose of this experiment involved me hiding from the chickens, then jumping out in front of or in back of them when they least expected it. The result was a lot of ruffled feathers, but no eggs popped from any chicken's backside.

While play with chickens provides some level of enjoyment, entertainment, and exercise, it was not producing the desired outcome. I was going to have to go deeper. In order to facilitate egg production, I needed to figure out where eggs come from. The easy answer to that question is a chicken. I checked that off the list, and returned to the oracle.

I do remember that at some point in my childhood, perhaps at age eight or nine, I went on an egg boycott. The boycott coincided with a lesson in school where we learned about egg development. The boycott lasted approximately six months – which is a significant period of time in the life of an eight-year-old. Eventually the disgust born from knowledge faded, and eggs once again found their way to my plate, fork, mouth, and belly. Unafraid of unintended consequences, I dove once more into the world of eggs.

Like human females, a chicken (hen) is born with a finite number of eggs, already inside her. Once the supply of eggs has been depleted, laying ceases. NOTE: menopause ends the laying capacity of female humans who lay an egg once a month and are born with more eggs than will ever be cycled through ovulation and menstruation.

Typically, chickens lay one egg a day, though it varies by breed. White egg birds will lay 260-285 eggs a year; brown egg layers 240-280 eggs a year. While it is impossible for a chicken to lay more than one egg a day, it is common for chickens to skip days, especially in fall and winter. The pineal gland, which sits behind the eyes, monitors and measures daylight. If there is sufficient light, the gland will send out a hormone triggering ovulation. As sunlight decreases, the hormone is withheld thus ceasing egg production.

The gland can be tricked with the introduction of artificial light, a practice that is readily employed by both commercial and backyard egg producers. A minimum of 12 hours of light is needed to keep production levels steady throughout the year.

Younger hens lay more regularly and are more likely to lay through winter, while older hens' eggs are usually larger. After laying for 10 months or so, hens usually take a break and molt their feathers before cycling up again. Total egg production will decrease annually. On average, most hens will lay out all their eggs within three to four years.

It takes 26 hours for an egg to be laid. As the University of Kentucky Extension Service details, the process begins in the ovary where there is an assembly line producing single celled ova each encased in a membrane that then develop into a yolk; a seven to nine-day process. When mature – the pineal gland signals that there is enough daylight – the yolk is released from the ovary in a process referred to as ovulation. It then drops into the hen's abdominal cavity where the outer lips of the oviduct grab hold and pull it inside.

Inside the oviduct which, is a tube 25-30 inches long and divided into five sections, the rest of the egg is formed. Stop number one on the skillet express is the infundibulum. Were fertilization to occur, this is where it would happen. Hens, like most birds, can take in, store, and then dispense sperm as needed.

It is important at this point to clear up what may be most misunderstood fact about chickens and eggs – and it is not which one came first. No. You do not need a rooster for hens to produce eggs, as I am more than happy to explain when asked. We women lay an egg every month, so to speak, without the assistance of any male. Without sperm, our eggs and the hens' eggs are simply unfertilized.

After 15 minutes in the infundibulum, the egg moves on to the next and largest section (13 inches in length) of the oviduct, the magnum, where it takes three hours for the albumen or egg white to form. Next it is off to the isthmus for 75 minutes. This is when and where the inner and outer shell membranes are added.

The penultimate section is the uterus where the egg spends 20 hours as the shell is formed. The egg is consistently rotated while in the uterus thereby ensuring an equal distribution of shell material. Forty seven percent of the calcium needed for shell production is synthesized from the hen's own bones. The balance comes from dietary inputs. Food for our layers is calcium rich and is also generally supplemented with crushed oyster shells. Our lucky chickens also get a healthy dose of calcium from their daily servings of yogurt. It is also here in the uterus where any pigment is added. NOTE: During the incubation of fertilized eggs, calcium from the shell is dissolved, taken up by the developing chick, and used in the formation of bones. This process makes the shell thinner and therefore, easier to escape when hatch time comes.

In addition to the shell formation, the chalsa is also formed while the egg is in the uterus. The chalsa consists of two cord-like structures which function to keep the yolk centered in the egg – not knocking around. If you look closely at a recently cracked egg, you may be able to see one or two stringy looking things. Many people remove the chalsa before cooking an egg, falsely believing it to be sperm left over from a rooster.

The final stop isn't really a stop at all. In fact, it is a push. The vagina's muscles work to expel the egg. The egg enters the vagina small side first, but is rotated so that the egg exits large side first. Eve's curse extended to our fine-feathered friends? As it exits, the egg gets that special antibacterial coating – the bloom. Thirty minutes later, the process begins again.

Chickens, like all birds have only one hole. They pee, poo, and lay eggs through a common opening known as the vent. This efficiency gave rise to the saying one would use to convince a friend that she can keep a secret, "I'm like a chicken, water goes in, but none comes out." Chickens cannot expel excrement and lay an egg at the same time. The vent has a gatekeeper referred to as the cloaca. Once the egg passes the cloaca, the gate shuts closing off the intestines.

Though I now had fascinating egg facts to share with friends and family, nothing I read provided any real guidance, hints or advice to advance egg production. I was back at square one. Two of the four chickens were laying, and it seemed there was nothing I could do but hope Mother Nature would cast a beneficent gaze upon Nicole and Glynn Ann before Christmas.

To make things worse, the two non-layers began to test my nerves and patience. On their daily walkabouts, Nicole had taken to straying from the designated forage areas into the garlic patch. Chris and I planted five different varieties of garlic that fall. The tender shoots were just starting to emerge from the ground. Not satisfied with the bushes next to the house, the two tiers of planting beds, or a vast carpet of lawn, whenever my back was turned, and even when I was looking directly at her, Nicole would make her way to the garlic patch and begin scratching through the recycled chicken bedding mulch, disturbing the innocent garlic.

Instead of a peaceful beginning and ending to my day, the daily walkabouts became a test of wills, Nicole's versus mine. It was a constant battle. I blocked her path, she went around. I chased her off with a stick, she returned. I chided her, she ignored me.

As if that weren't bad enough, Glynn Ann began to resist going back into the coop in the evening or the annex in the morning. No amount of yogurt or fresh vegetables, bread, or grits, could pull her away from the yard. The other three would be safe and sound in either the annex or the coop, but Glynn Ann continued happily pecking away at a log, bush or a patch of dirt. I am all for happy chickens, but I would be happier if the chickens behaved.

Nicole and Glynn Ann were doing nothing to curry favor. They were playing a dangerous game – one where there would be no winners.

A few days before Christmas, with my nerves plucked, I dutifully donned a winter coat, hat, and gloves, and made my way out in the frigid morning to let the chickens out. I collected one blue egg from the coop, plopped it in a pocket, and commenced to play Words with Friends. After scoring a seven-letter word worth 95 points, I looked up. Sure enough, Nicole was over in the garlic patch. Furious, I trekked over and as I reached for the long stick that separates the different varieties of garlic from one another, it happened. Nicole squatted.

Before announcing to Chris the impending delivery of an egg, I had to be sure. I waited a bit then   approached Nicole again. Instead of running away, she squatted. Chris would have to grant a reprieve. What better Christmas gift to receive than an egg. What better Christmas gift to give than life. The remaining hold out was Glynn Ann. Nicole had saved herself, but would it be enough to save Glynn Ann?

Armed with my new egg knowledge and visual confirmation of multiple Nicole squats, I confronted Chris. It's not that Chris was in any way, shape, or form, eager to kill a chicken. Her argument was firmly rooted in economics, not emotion. She was overjoyed with the news of Nicole, and we both hoped that her egg would be a Christmas miracle/breakfast.

As for Glynn Ann, I spun her delayed egg production as a positive. There are eggs inside that hen, and they will come out, I explained. When Todd and Ellen run out of eggs, Nicole and Glynn Ann, will still be laying thereby extending the total egg production when measured on a time scale. Chris is nothing if not reasonable. The argument made sense, and she agreed keep the flock intact.

The argument did, however, beg another question. What

happens after the chickens run out of eggs?

Nicole did not lay on Christmas morning, afternoon or evening. She did eventually lay an egg on December 28, 2011 – which was eaten for breakfast on January 2, 2012 by the human Todd, who was visiting from Chicago. Glynn Ann began squatting on January 20, 2012.

Oh Snow

As fall fell into winter, so too did the temperatures and then the snow. Though we made sure to select cold-tolerant varieties of chickens, we weren't exactly sure just how cold-tolerant they would be. The literature all seemed to indicate that they would fare just fine. But what do the experts know?

Before things got too cold, Chris and I moved the coop from its summer location under the protective shade of trees, to its new winter location on the other side of the yard away from trees in the direct pathway of the sun to take advantage of natural thermal energy.

Then it happened. Temperatures plummeted. We were terrified. The first night of freezing temperatures, I was frantically scouring the internet for guidance. The one piece of information I found and took to heart was to not install a heat lamp inside of the coop. Each year, chickeneers with the best of intentions do just that, only to awake to a conflagration of burning flesh and feathers.

Since there was no way I could not do something and get any amount of sleep, I settled on insulation. I gathered up five or so blankets and sleeping bags and proceeded to layer them one on top of each other on top of the coop. If I woke up the next morning to find four frozen chickens, I would at least be absolved of some level of guilt for having done something.

Next morning, I pulled the wet frozen mass of blankets from the coop, opened the door, and found four very alive chickens. They had survived. But the temperatures continued to drop.

Perhaps it is my own personal aversion to coldness that

compelled me to ensure that the chickens would be warm. The next night, in addition to the blankets, I added hot water bottles filled with nearly boiling water, wrapped in towels and placed inside the roosting box with the chickens. Again, they survived. Thinking we were helping to keep them alive, Chris and I kept up this nightly routine.

Then the snow came. With the yard blanketed in white, I opened the coop door. Ellen tentatively stepped out onto the frozen landscape then quickly hopped back into the coop. Following Ellen's lead, the other three stayed inside.

Getting to and from the coop became a treacherous exercise but one that had to be done. Like all living beings, chickens need water to survive. With the temperatures at or below freezing all day, their water quickly became ice thus requiring Chris or myself to regularly change out the frozen water containers with liquid counterparts.

We soon realized that we had a natural insulator, so we abandoned the blankets for the layer of snow. Then, on a particularly nasty winter night, the hot water bottles did not make it into the coop. And still the girls survived thus ending our irrational attempts to artificially maintain the coop at a comfortable temperature. Their methods were far superior.

Here we were worrying about our chickens, as well we should, but not making any connection to the resident wild birds whose territory we share. The blue jay and dove survive through the winter without the aid of humans. Why would our chickens be any different? Answer is, they are not.

Birds are able to survive freezing temperatures thanks to their feathers. The average chicken has about 8,000 feathers (predictably, the bird with the most feathers is the tundra swan with 25,000). In winter, the layers of feathers are fluffed up creating air pockets that capture the heat produced by the birds' bodies. Less than an inch of feathered insulation can keep a bird a toasty 104 degrees. Ironically, it is an excess of heat rather than an excess of cold that provides the greatest threat to bird/chicken health.

My fears allayed, I slept like a chicken under a goose down comforter until spring.

Lame Duck Chicken

Back while we were waiting for the chickens to arrive, Chris and I read books and blogs, trying to acquire the necessary knowledge needed to effectively raise chickens. To give them a better chance for survival, we also sprang for immunizations against common chicken diseases – an extra $.50 per chick. All the research and immunizations must have paid off. All four chickens successfully navigated the transition from chick to pullet to hen without any health issues. All streaks, however, must come to an end as did this one when the flock was visited by injury.

One evening, as cocktail hour approached, I prepared the daily chicken martini and headed outside for some free-range scratching and exploring. I opened the gate to the annex and Todd, Ellen, and Glynn Ann flew the coop and began foraging. Nicole, anxious for free play, stood up and began limping her way out of the annex. She was hurt.

I closed the gate to keep Nicole quarantined, and called out to Chris "chicken down!" We took the cover off of the annex to gain entry and scooped up Nicole for a closer look. She was favoring her right foot so that is where the examination began. We looked for the obvious, cuts, or a splinter. Unfortunately, the examination quickly stalled. Nicole's right foot was caked with poop. Using a small stick, Chris gently tried to pluck the poop off of Nicole's foot. But the extent of poop intrusion was so great, that we had to engage a different technique.

While the other three chickens amused themselves in the yard, Chris and I took Nicole inside the house. Rather than squawking disapproval, Nicole radiated a calm demeanor. There was no wing flapping or squirming to get free. The only movement came from Nicole's head as she strained in a very inquisitive manner to assess the interior design choices made for the basement game room and workshop.

At the basement sink, we filled a bowl with warm water and dipped Nicole's foot in to dislodge the remaining poop from her foot. A chicken's foot is a topographer's nightmare. We searched every crease and crevice, but there were no obvious cuts or splinters to be found. The investigation then moved from the external to the internal. I held Nicole as Chris began to gently apply pressure to each foot and leg joint. No matter where we poked, pressed, or prodded, Nicole did not utter any cries of pain. The source of the limping remained a mystery. With human first aid exhausted, we returned Nicole to the flock. We would wait to see if the limp got better or worse overnight.

As Nicole settled into the coop for the night, I began a determined search for causes and cures for a limping chicken. Into the Google search box I typed, "limping chicken." To my utter surprise, up popped pages and pages of blog and chat room entries with titles like, "Help. My chicken is limping." We were not alone.

The first entry I read was from another suburban chicken farmer whose chicken was limping badly. Like us, she had searched for external causes and had found none. Like Nicole, the chicken seemed to be expressing limited signs of pain and had continued to eat normally. However, she ended the entry with a thought that had heretofore not crossed my mind. The woman explained that, even though it would be a hard choice, she wanted to know whether or not to kill the chicken to put it out of its misery.

Panic took hold. Adrenaline started to flow. My mind raced. Life on the farm, as we all learned at a young age through the story of Charlotte's Web, is cruel. Life and death decisions must be made. But we have created an artificial distance between us and the food that is served on our plates and where that food comes from. It is this distance that the local food revolution is trying to bridge. I have always found it easy to step up on the nearest soapbox (I carry one around in my purse) and preach on any number of topics, including the fact that if one eats meat, then one should at one point kill an animal prior to eating it. But now one of my girls was injured and I felt that old friend hypocrisy slowly creeping in.

My words were coming home to roost. Faced with making the hard decision, who would do the killing? Nicole was my friend, so it stood to reason that I should wield the axe. Although I would rely upon Chris to hold the body firm to the ground. It wouldn't seem right just to throw some mushroom soup on top of Nicole and stick her in the oven. No. Great thought would have to go into deciding upon, and then preparing, the dish or dishes Nicole's body would provide. And then, who would eat Nicole? Would Chris and I sit down by ourselves with a bottle of wine and toast Nicole upon each bite or should we invite friends and family to join in the meal, making it more of a party?

Luckily the responses to the woman's inquiry staunched the flow of adrenaline and refocused my mind to the problem at hand   Nicole's limp. Others who had experienced limping chickens implored the woman not to rush to the kill. Some explained that they have healthy and happy chickens that just happen to limp. Others provided various assessments and remedies. One person swore by brewer's yeast. Another suggested dissolving aspirin into the drinking water. Still another described her husband performing physical therapy on their limping chicken. He would hold the chicken with its legs barely touching the ground and walk it around the yard.

The brewer's yeast and aspirin seemed to show up on a more or less consistent basis on a variety of websites dedicated to chicken health. They were associated remedies for sprains. Hoping that Nicole's injury fell into the sprain category, Chris and I made a plan to feed Nicole a special batch of grits with brewer's yeast mixed in, and dissolve some aspirin into the flock's drinking water. And just in case we missed a cut or scrape during the physical examination, we would do as one online post suggested and dip the foot into a bowl of hydrogen peroxide to see if it bubbles.

The websites also provided information on non-sprain related causes for a limping chicken; the two most prominent causes being bumblefoot, an infection found on the feet of birds, and Marek's Disease, a contagious viral disease that causes internal lesions and kills more chickens than any other disease. We ruled out Marek's disease because Nicole was not exhibiting the "down in the leg" paralysis form of limping associated with the disease. Bumblefoot was also ruled out after we combed through hundreds of images showing the infection.

The next morning when I let the chickens out, Nicole was still limping. The limp had not gotten any better, but it seemed not to have gotten any worse. Chris and I dunked Nicole's foot into a hydrogen peroxide bath. There were bubbles. Could it be that there was just a tiny cut or sliver imbedded in her foot that we couldn't see that was causing the limp? For added precaution, one 85 mg aspirin was dissolved into a gallon of water and fed to all of the chickens. Just in case Nicole's injury was affecting her appetite, we made sure she got a dose of the meds by hand-feeding her water using a pipette. I also cooked up a batch of grits, half for my own breakfast augmented with bacon and cheese. The other half for the chickens augmented with brewer's yeast.

I kept a watchful eye on Nicole throughout the day. Again, she spent the majority of the day in a seated position, perched on top of the laying box. When she wasn't sitting, she was finding her way to the feed bowl. She still had an appetite; a good sign.

We repeated the procedures the next day. First Nicole's foot was dunked into hydrogen peroxide; again eliciting bubbles. Another round of aspirin water was loaded into the flock's water supply for the day. Nicole rested her foot, only putting pressure on it when hunger trumped pain.

That afternoon when the chickens were let out for free range time, Nicole's limp wasn't as pronounced. Hope took hold. Something was working. Nicole was on the mend. It took two more days until Nicole was jumping and flying and running around the yard like a chicken with her head on once again. The axe and recipe book still lay at the ready, but in the meantime, all was quiet down on the farm.

Tastes Like Chicken

I'm not sure who to contact about changing an idiom, but I feel strongly that the saying, "it's a dog eat dog world" should be changed to, "it's a chicken eat chicken world." Chickens are cannibalistic. Apparently, it has something to do with blood. They love blood. Just when you thought it was safe to go into the coop. The sight of blood on another chicken will cause the non-bleeding chickens to peck until death and beyond. I have read reports of inter-flock cannibalism where all that was left of the chicken was a pile of bones and feathers.

Before I continue, I should let you know that my foray into the darker side of chicken rearing was not predicated by actual cannibalism within the family per say, but cannibalism lite, chickens eating their eggs.

In the first incident, Ellen was the perpetrator. Whenever I was home during the day and noticed one of the chickens doing the "I need to lay" dance, which closely resembles a child's, "I need to pee" dance, I trekked down to the annex, grabbed the chicken, and moved it into the coop for a little private time. It is a bit indulgent, I admit. But they seemed to prefer to lay in the coop more than in the annex. On the day in question, both Todd and Ellen were visibly agitated and needing to lay. I moved both into the coop. An hour or so later, I went out to check on their progress. Todd had laid a beautiful blue egg. Ellen had not. I congratulated Todd on her egg and moved her back into the annex with Nicole and Glynn Ann, but left Todd's egg in the coop with Ellen.

Another hour transpired. I walked out to the coop to check

on Ellen. Where once there had been one egg, now there was none. That's not entirely true. There were a few bits and pieces of blue egg shell along with a tiny bit of egg white slime – telltale signs of the crime. I was furious. After a few choice words, I moved Ellen back into the annex then proceeded to remove any and all vestiges of the destroyed egg from the coop.

Knowing Ellen's proclivity for bad behavior, I simply resolved to never again leave her alone with another egg. End of story. Not quite.

A few weeks later, I happened to look outside of the kitchen window and noticed two brown eggs sitting inside the laying box. Way to go Glynn Ann and Nicole. Something inside me told me to go get the eggs right then and there. Something else inside me – the procrastination gene - said to wait. I opted to wait. That decision proved to be ill-fated.

When it was time to let the girls out for their evening forage, I noted with extreme displeasure that where once there were two eggs, there was but one. This time the remaining evidence of the carnage included an almost intact egg. The top quarter had been compromised, and the entire contents of the egg removed – consumed by one or more of the chickens. Based on her previous behavior, I pointed the finger at Ellen. But really it could have been any one of them or a combination thereof.

With two known incidents of egg eating, I now had to wonder how many other eggs had suffered the same fate only with the chickens doing a better job at concealing the evidence. It didn't matter. Two was too many given the time and effort Chris and I had invested in production. This had to stop.

I typed into the oracle, "Help. My chickens are eating their eggs." With one click of the mouse, I again found that I was not alone. There were hundreds of similar inquiries posted on dozens of backyard chicken list servers.

I discovered that egg eating by chickens is a widespread problem. One person noted that she was experiencing a 50% loss in her flock of 15. Ironically, many people regularly feed their chickens crushed chicken eggs as a calcium supplement. The key is to crush the egg shells so completely that they in no way, shape or form resemble an egg. You have to be careful to clean the shells of all yolk and egg white material as well. Because chickens will acquire a taste for eggs and they will continue to seek them out. The behavior is also contagious. Chickens learn from one another. Ellen may have been at fault initially, but we ran the chance that the others would learn from the ringleader thus leading to even more destruction.

Many of the posted solutions to this problem involve teaching chickens to despise eggs by filling them with combinations of hot sauce and mustard. These techniques are, however, more wives tale than fact. Chickens taste food quite differently than humans. Whereas we would probably never eat another egg again if it tasted of mustard and hot sauce, the same flavor combination would have no effect on the chickens. Chickens have between 20-500 taste buds. Humans have 10,000.

The experts overwhelmingly agree that egg consumption by chickens is caused by boredom. Chickens sense the world through their beaks. If they aren't sleeping, they are pecking. They peck at everything. Without any other stimulating material to peck, they will undoubtedly turn their attention to eggs. Then it is a viscous circle. Out of boredom, they peck at an egg, find that they like it, and continue to peck at eggs. Apparently, our chickens didn't share the same reverence Chris and I do for their eggs.

So now, in addition to general care and feeding of the chickens, I had to find ways to stimulate the flock. You would think that they were laying golden eggs.

Chris and I had been meaning to add a mirror to the annex for months. Being good chicken parents means keeping up to date on the latest chicken parenting trends.

The egg eating moved that process forward. I found a broken piece of mirror in a construction dumpster, brought it home and propped it up along one side of the annex. The excitement level within the flock rose immediately. Normally, my mere presence near the annex draws everyone's attention because it usually means food. When I walk through the yard, all eyes are generally fixed on me. Not anymore.

All eyes turned to the mirror. They were transfixed. I'm not sure if they recognized themselves staring back or just thought that four new chickens had joined the flock. I like to think it was the former. They all huddled around the looking glass for hours that first day. As the days went on, it was rare to see all four huddled in front of the mirror at once. Rather it just became Ellen. Which was fine with me. As long as she was admiring herself in the mirror, she wasn't destroying any eggs.

The mirror was a good addition, but I wasn't going to place all of my eggs into one basket. We needed more, so golf balls made another appearance. This time, the faux eggs were meant to frustrate. Their unbreakable composition is meant to make the act of pecking at an egg one of futility. I also threw in a variety of brightly colored dog toys. Feed companies also make blocks of feed which are designed to give the chickens something to work on throughout the course of a day. Being cheap, I started putting large decomposing logs full of insects into the annex for the same effect.

However, the quest to save the eggs did not stop at mere distraction techniques. This was an all-of-the-above, multi-faceted strategy. Since chickens don't like to eat in the dark, Chris added a curtained flap to close off the open side of the laying box, but still allow easy ingress and egress. I was dubious, thinking that the curtain would limit usage of the laying box. I was wrong. Each day, one by one, the chickens went into the box, laid their eggs and exited.

They also no longer squawked or did the "I have to lay" dance.

Egg production rose. While we had yet to have a four-egg day, finding three eggs was becoming a regular occurrence. However, there was, and I guess will always be that nagging question – were some eggs still being eaten? No matter what you do, chickens will continue to be chickens. You can only hope that you raised them right.

There was one other suggestion provided on one of the online discussion threads. You take an egg and crack it open amongst the chickens. The first chicken to go to the egg and begin eating is your ringleader. Take the ringleader, roll it in flour and pepper, fry in oil, and consume.

Chicken Hawk

In nature, there are the hunters and the hunted. Each day the carnival of carnage plays itself out in large and small battles of wits, each side trying to outdo the other. It's a high-stakes game, not built for the faint of heart. To the victor goes dinner. To the loser, goes the grave. Both contestants come equipped with tools uniquely designed to either kill or evade. These tools are constantly being sharpened and upgraded through the processes called natural selection and evolution.

Chickens are both predator and prey. As omnivores, they eat just about anything, except the leaves of a cherry tree which can kill them. Using their large reptilian-like feet, they scratch at the ground trying to unearth unsuspecting grubs, worms, and insects. Their claws and sharp beak are their tools – and effective ones at that. They are, however, no match for determined predators.

Humans probably consume more chickens than any other animal. In the U.S. alone, we consume nearly 60 pounds of chicken per person, per year. But we are not the only animal that includes chicken in its consumption regime. The list of chicken-vores is long and varied and includes: coyotes, raccoons, foxes, weasels and their relatives, opossums, skunks, rodents, snakes, domestic animals such as dogs and cats, and of course birds of prey like hawks, and owls.

It wasn't always so that hawks preyed on chickens. A long, long time ago, back when "chicken had teeth," the hawk and the chicken were not mortal enemies. But, according to legend, that all changed when a hen – isn't it always the girl's fault? – got between the two.

One day, the hawk was flying about on the air currents, hardly moving its wings, when it spotted the most beautiful hen he had ever seen. He swooped down to the farmyard to get a better look. He perched on a fence post (hawks don't like to walk on the ground if they don't have to) and he called out in his best voice. The hen approached. His heart was at once overcome by her beauty and he asked her to marry him. To both of their surprise, she accepted. A dowry of corn was negotiated with the hen's parents and paid in full by the hawk. The two then flew off to start a life together.

However, at the neighboring farm lived a rooster who had longed for that same hen his whole life. Upon hearing of the marriage between the hen and the hawk, the rooster set off to try to win the heart of the hen. When he arrived at their home, the rooster pranced and strutted around the hen, as roosters will do to impress the ladies. At first the hen was emotionally torn between the two. But finally, unable to resist the lure of the cock, she left the hawk and returned to the farm with the cuckold rooster.

Furious, the hawk flew to the farm and demanded that the hen's parents repay the dowry. They were poor, had already spent the whole of the dowry and had no way to secure the compensation that was due the hawk. Seeking redress, the hawk elevated the case to the king. After hearing the story, the king sided with the hawk and awarded him royal permission to forever feed upon the children of the rooster. So from that day to this day, the hawk and the chicken have lived as enemies.

Ironically, the victory of the hawk over the chicken led to a steep decline in the hawk population, because it woke the heretofore sleeping giant, man. When hawk and chicken were friends, man, in the guise of the farmer, had complete and total dominion over the fate of his flock. Now that hawk had permission to eat chicken, he became man's competitor and the tables turned with the former hunter becoming the hunted.

Armed with rifles shooting bullets that cut through the air faster than a hawk's wing, man set about to kill hawks on sight, in order to protect his flock and dietary source of protein. All but the smallest of hawks gained the negative title of "chicken hawk." Considered only as a foe by the farmer, hawks were and are, in fact, also friends because the majority of their diet consists of small rodents which are apt to plague a farmer's fields and stores.

The killing of hawks was not limited to farmers. Hunters of small game fowl – also part of the hawks' diet – proceeded with great skill to try to decimate their competition through direct, lethal lead poisoning. Hawks were not the only bird of prey humans considered to be a threat. Eagles were referred to as the "wolves of the sky." So pervasive was the all-out attack on birds of prey that many species were hunted to the brink of extinction which ultimately precipitated the enactment of new laws protecting these aerial hunters.

While laws now prohibit humans from killing birds of prey, that age-old law decreed by that long-ago king allowing hawks to eat all the rooster's children is still in effect.

The prehistoric claws function as useful tools to the chicken-as-predator. But it is the placement of their eyes, one on one side of the head and one on the other, that helps the chicken-as-prey evade capture by hawks. This eyeball configuration allows chickens 300 degrees of visibility – helpful in spotting predators.

Chickens, like most birds, have a highly developed sense of hearing. Why else then would birds sing? Chickens have nearly 30 different vocalizations which they begin hearing and recognizing while still in the egg. Vocalization is how a mother hen keeps track of her brood, how a rooster directs the flock to good things to eat (roosters also trick hens into mating by issuing a food call when in fact there is no food), and how chickens warn each other of impending danger.

Our backyard chickens have their own expanded vocabulary that includes the, "what took you so long," "where's my yogurt," and "clean the damn coop" calls. And a few days ago, I learned with no uncertainty a new vocalization, one passed down from chicken to chicken ever since that rooster ran off with the beautiful hen – "HAWK!"

All four of the girls were enjoying a late afternoon dirt bath, purring in contentment as they swam through the loose soil taking care of their personal hygiene. When engaged in this particular form of ablution, they are 100% committed to the bath. I can then take a break from keeping the chickens out of view of the neighbors (we have no way of knowing if they are members of the pro, anti, or ambivalent chicken camps) and out of the garlic patch. After a good thirty minutes or so, they were still at it. With their outside forage time coming to a close, I dropped my guard and went to prepare their yogurt.

Unbeknownst to me, a hawk was circling high above the yard surveying the scene below. No sooner was I out of sight when the hawk made its move. I didn't see it coming. But I knew when it arrived. There was suddenly a great cacophony of squawks and flapping feathers. I looked up and there was only one bird in sight. It was the hawk, perched on the deck overlooking the coop a mere 10 feet away. The chickens were nowhere to be seen.

I was confused, perplexed. As my mind tried to wrap itself around the attack, I stood in awe of the great bird. Its talons were empty. This was a good sign. My awe soon turned to ire. I leaped up from behind the barbeque pit and the hawk flew to a nearby tree. I kept advancing, shouting and flailing my arms like a giant flightless bird. The hawk took to the sky empty handed. However, he now knew where we lived.

With the hawk out of the picture, I searched the yard for the chickens. Todd and Ellen had scooted under the deck while Nicole and Glynn Ann sought refuge in the bushes. 1, 2, 3, 4. All were alive and accounted for.

One of the 30 chicken vocalizations is the "all clear" signal. I was only beginning to talk chicken and had not yet learned that one, so I said it in English. The chickens seemed to understand and furtively came out of hiding. I ran down to fetch the yogurt to help persuade them to go into the coop for the evening. No such persuasion was necessary. They ran as quickly as their legs could carry them across the open and exposed portion of the yard into the coop. I double checked that all the hatches were securely fastened, placed the container of yogurt in the coop, and bid them a good night.

The next morning, I chanced a peek outside the kitchen window. There perched high upon a limb of a tree with a direct view into the coop, was the hawk. Almost an hour passed, and when I looked out the window again, the hawk was still there. This bird was no birdbrain. Even when I walked outside, to better gauge the situation, he did not move. I was up against a pretty formidable foe.

At regular intervals throughout the day, I walked outside and scanned the skies and neighboring trees for any sight of the hawk. Once the coast was clear, as far as I could see it, life regained its normal rhythm. The birds foraged in the morning and the evenings (though I kept a more watchful eye), spent their days in the annex and their nights in the coop. All was quiet on the suburban farm, until it wasn't.

A few weeks later, on an unseasonably warm day in February, I heard some strange and distressing sounds coming from the annex. It was a large and guttural, "ba ba ba ba ba BAWK!" At first, I didn't give it much thought. As it continued, I began to worry, and rightfully so. The hawk was back, and this time he brought a friend.

Two hawks glided over and around the yard, their shadows seemingly the size of 747's. They circled and perched, circled and perched, letting out blood-curdling whistle shrieks that brought out my own inner fowl in the form of goose-pimples. The chickens weren't exactly sitting ducks, protected on all sides by the metal mesh of the annex, but that was little consolation. They were terrified, and I was unable to assuage their fear or discourage the hawks from their pursuits. All we could do was wait it out.

After forty-five minutes or so, the hawks either gave up or lost interest and went away. A week elapsed, and no hawks were sighted. An uneasy calm has once again settled in the backyard. While I would like to think this is the end of the story, I know it is not. Nature ain't beanbag. The hawks will be back because as Henery Hawk, the little chicken hawk from Looney Tunes sings:

(Chicken Hawk, gettin' hungry)
(Chicken Hawk, gettin' hungry)
I want some chicken, to eat.
It is my favorite meat.
I like it crispy or glazed.
It puts me in a daze.
I like it fried up or baked.
On my birthday I eat chicken cake!
(Chicken Hawk's not a chicken)
(He's just a hawk that eats chicken)
Now, just one second, all right?
I've got something for your appetite.
There's so many things that you could eat.
There's a Chinese restaurant down the street.
Or how about a fish taco, son?
This bakery's got a good honey bun.
So juicy...so tasty...
Hey chicken, get in my mouth!
How about a hot dog?
With mustard and Sauerkraut.
NO!

I want some chicken no lie.
You are my chicken pot pie.
Instead of chicken try pork.
Just please put down that fork.
Try my grandma's baked beans.
They've got 10 grams of protein.
They're gooey, sweet, and piping hot.
You'll wanna eat the whole dang pot.
(Chicken Hawk, gonna eat the beans)
(Chicken Hawk is enjoying them beans)
I knew you'd come around, son.
You know what would go good with these beans?
Chicken.
Uh-oh.
Get over here chicken

I'm Coming Out

Spring came early to Maryland that year. Mild temperatures coupled with longer days quickly transformed the browns and grays of the landscape into bright greens and pastels. The cherry blossoms in DC bloomed before the official start of the annual cherry blossom festival. Warmed by the sun, dormant or hibernating animals stirred, and the earth woke quickly after a long winter's nap.

It was the chickens' first spring and they suffered from a severe bout of Ferris Bueller-like spring fever. They weren't content in the coop or in the annex or in the middle of the yard. Presented with a world bursting with new culinary offerings, the girls pushed geographic boundaries and with it the patience of their humans.

Not content with scratching in the bushes near the house, the chickens flew, ran and hopped from one end of the yard to the other. With a trusty four-foot dowel in hand, I ran around the yard trying to keep the flock together. If one broke free, usually Glynn Ann, I was forced to run after her, leaving the other three unattended. Sensing an opportunity, the three unattended chickens would run off to one or the other sides of the lawn bordering the neighbors.

Despite continuous effort on the part of backyard chicken advocates, the law in Baltimore County remained and remains unchanged. These chickens were outlaws.

Though bursting with buds, the trees still lacked full foliage leaving gapped viewscapes from yard to yard. Spring also pulled powerfully on the human inhabitants of the neighborhood. Lawnmowers fired up, mulch was spread, barbeque pits came on line.

We might have been perfectly safe. Our neighbors maybe were all secret chicken lovers. But then again, maybe not. It wasn't a chance that Chris or I were willing to take. But the chickens had other ideas. They were either braver or just plain bird-brained, but they insisted on foraging along the property lines, rather than close to the house or in the middle of the yard.

Did they want to be spotted? Did they want to come out of the shadows? Did they want to be on the front lines of the back-yard chicken revolution? Or like everyone else, did they just believe the grass is greener on the other side? Which, by the way it isn't. Thanks to their prolific pooping, our grass was pretty damn green.

Despite our best efforts at concealment, the first chink in the armor was finally realized. Chris was out with the chickens. Unable to do just one thing at a time, she watched the chickens, played Words with Friends, weeded the garden, and worked at construct-ing a new compost bin. The neighbor to our north was out and about busying himself with some yard work. He saw Chris and walked over to say hi. Chris was trapped. There was nothing she could do, but come out. "We have chickens," she blurted. "I know" was the response.

It seems that a few weeks back, the neighbor had been up on his roof, cleaning out the gutters. He happened to look over into our yard and saw something out of the ordinary. After a few min-utes of careful observation, he surmised that what he was seeing were chickens. The discovery did not elicit any antagonism or legal procedures. We didn't know that he knew, and he didn't think it necessary to call attention to the matter.

Chris sighed in relief. However, there were three more sets of neighbors. Did they know, or didn't they? It was anyone's guess (and still is). The chickens didn't make things any easier. We hoped that summer would come early to Maryland as well, and the hot, humid temperatures would slow their appetite for exploration, and they would be content with simply sitting in the shade sipping on iced tea.

The Early Bird Gets the Worm

I not only didn't think it was possible, the thought never once crossed my mind. There are things no one, and I mean no one, should be forced to see. This was one of those things.

The day was like any other day. I woke up, fixed myself a cup of coffee and headed out to tend the chickens. The day would warm up into the sixties, but it was a chilly morning. Fog blanketed the yard, the ground was moist. The girls were anxious to be let out, stretch their wings, and get their scratch on. They tore out of the coop, and immediately began gorging on the fresh sprigs of grass and clover.

Their attention soon turned. First one, then another, until finally all four were pulling worms out of the ground. I didn't think much of it at first. The ground was wet, worms live in the ground. It was spring, the worms, like the rest of the earth were emerging from winter's grasp. I was happy for the chickens. They love worms. I was happy also that now I didn't have to dig up worms for them to enjoy as a treat. But these were not the type of earthworms with which I was familiar. These were monstrous creatures, their diameter the size of an adult index finger. Their length upwards of fourteen inches. These, I would come to learn, were nightcrawlers.

Nightcrawlers are a type of earthworm. Their size and ability to stay alive for five minutes when immersed in water make them prized as fishing bait. As such, nightcrawlers are regularly hunted, yes hunted. Flashlights are used to find the crawlers who crawl partially out of their holes to sprawl on the grass. Once located, the hunters extinguish the light, drop to the ground, and stealthily begin crawling towards the prey. When in reach, they pin the crawler to the ground with one hand while grasping the body at a spot nearest the tunnel with the other, not yanking or squeezing too hard, but patiently waiting out the crawler's initial instinctual contractions. It eventually relaxes, making extraction easy.

Like their human counterparts, chickens also hunt nightcrawlers but in a different, albeit very effective manner. Using their beaks, they quickly grab hold of the crawler and pull. My observations revealed that thirty-three percent of the time, the crawler escapes the initial contact. Thirty-three percent of the time, the chicken is able to extract only one piece of the crawler, usually an inch or so. And thirty-three percent of the time, the entire worm is captured.

On those occasions where the chicken has successfully extracted an entire nightcrawler from its hole, the first course of business is to move the worm as far away from the hole – its escape route – as possible. The second challenge is to position the crawler for consumption. By now however, one or more of the other chickens will have realized that one of its feathered friends is in possession of a full length nightcrawler, and they will attempt to steal the prize.

It really is anyone's game at this point. The nightcrawler may pass between two or more chickens prior to final consumption. In the process, the nightcrawler is almost always torn up into smaller and smaller pieces as it is consumed by multiple birds. However, there are other times when one bird alone, consumes the whole nightcrawler.

This is truly something to behold. Things have to line up just right for this to happen. The chicken needs enough time away from the other birds to effectively position the worm at an angle conducive to full throat consumption. Think slurping a long piece of spaghetti into your mouth. Now replace the spaghetti with a fourteen-inch-long hotdog – for that more closely approximates the beak to diameter ratio realized when a chicken eats a nightcrawler.

While mildly disturbing, the daily struggle between chicken and worm is one that fits neatly within accepted norms of nature. Accepted norms that would be shattered a mere eight hours later during the evening's regular forage when all hell broke loose.

At first, I thought the hawks were back. I scanned the skies, but saw nothing. Then I saw that Glynn Ann had something in her mouth, and all the other chickens wanted it. Since I don't normally intervene in those kinds of squabbles, I turned my mind back to day dreaming. However, the fighting intensified to a level that I could no longer ignore. At that point, Glynn Anne hopped off the terraced garden back into the yard with the coveted something dangling from her mouth. I took a closer look and discovered it was a mouse.

Glynn Anne had dug up a sleeping mouse, now dead. Was she going to eat this? Do chickens eat mice? Apparently, they do, because the other three chickens chased Glynn Ann around the yard, squawking and pecking at her to gain possession of the prize. I joined in the chase, thinking for some reason that I needed to get the mouse because it couldn't possibly be right for them to have it. Glynn Anne wasn't relinquishing control of the mouse to me or any of the other chickens. I gave up.

Nicole, Todd, and Ellen continued. Every couple of seconds or so, Glynn Anne stopped, hacked at the mouse, then moved along, pecked a little more, picked up the mouse, and continued to elude Todd, Nicole, and Ellen. She devoured the head first. Then cutting through the skin, began on the internal organs. This is where the others were able to take advantage of the situation. Internal organs poured out all over the yard. While Glynn Ann maintained control over most of the carcass, the other chickens picked up whatever dropped. Todd was able to pry away a leg, and content with that, left the chase. Nicole was Glynn Anne's greatest adversary. Near the end of the melee, Nicole ripped a third of the body away from Glynn Anne, and swallowed it in two mighty bites.

Shocked, dismayed, disgusted, intrigued, I stood there watching the macabre ballet play out before my eyes. The question is why was this so disturbing? Chickens are omnivores. If it had been a raptor, any other bird of prey or a cat even, feasting on a mouse, I would not have had any visceral reaction. Animals are hard-wired to eat or not eat certain things. Their unfettered exuberance at the sight of the mouse was evidence that chickens have been eating mice for a long, long time, evolutionarily speaking.

Why is it easier to accept eating chicken eggs fortified by worms as opposed to eggs fortified by a mouse? Maybe it's just that I never thought, or had to think about the full and natural dietary inclinations of a chicken. Maybe I am just over thinking the whole thing, and should simply enjoy that omelet with mushrooms, bacon, cheese and mouse.

Chicken Scratch

Chris and I had just finished laying four inches of mulch throughout the garden. Not only was it aesthetically pleasing but we figured that the mulch would dissuade the chickens from rummaging in the garden. Our chicken assumptions were once again proven wrong. Even with a whole yard of interesting pecking grounds, the chickens loved nothing better than to scratch down through the fresh mulch leaving unappealing pockmarks in the landscaping, much to Chris' displeasure.

This habit traces back – if you believe in folk tales – to one day when all of the farm animals were invited to a dinner party thrown by cat and dog.

Like chicken and hawk, cat and dog were still friends at the time. Rooster, who with his brilliant plumage, thought himself highly superior to all of the other animals, accepted the dinner invitation with a caveat. He would show up to the feast, if and only if said feast was to be a tremendous affair with multiple courses. In short, the feast had to be as great as he thought himself to be. Cat and dog promised a feast like no other.

At the appointed time, all of the animals gathered at the lavish table, but rooster was nowhere to be found. Wanting to make a grand entrance, rooster planned on arriving fashionably late. So as not to be rude, all of the animals waited patiently for the arrival of roster before beginning to eat. When rooster finally arrived, he surveyed the table. In front of each animal stood a plate dominated by a huge slab of cornbread.

"Cornbread" the rooster said indignantly. "I thought this was going to be a feast worthy of my presence. I can get all the corn-bread I want at home." With that, the rooster turned, gave a few insulting huffs, and walked out. As he pranced away, he couldn't help but hear loud shouts of joy and excitement emanating from the table. He turned ever so slightly and saw that underneath the slab of corn bread was layer upon layer of vegetables and sweets. Too proud to admit that he was wrong, the rooster had no other choice but to continue his retreat. From that time hence, even if food is lying in plain sight, rooster will scratch at the ground to make sure nothing is hiding underneath.

No One Can Eat 50 Eggs

As the weather continued to warm and the days lengthen, egg production continued to ramp up. Four-egg days were becoming the norm. That equates to one dozen eggs every three days. This level of production prompted us to come up with new and interesting ways of consuming eggs. It is fortunate that eggs are so versatile; boiled (hard and soft), sunny side up, over easy, over hard, scrambled, poached, baked in a quiche or frittata, used to make mayonnaise or aioli, and a primary component of baked goods.

In spite of all these uses, there seemed to always come a point when our little brass egg basket sitting on the kitchen counter began to overflow. Visions circulated in our brains of that iconic scene in the classic movie, "Cool Hand Luke" where Paul Newman challenges himself to eat 50 eggs in one hour. When faced with an overflow, Chris or I headed down to the basement, grabbed an empty egg carton, filled it with eggs, and delivered them as gifts to friends and neighbors. Good fences make good neighbors, so do good eggs.

One weekend as we packed our suitcases to head down to New Orleans to help celebrate human Ellen's 50th birthday, I saw that our supply of eggs was ample. So, I thought why not bring some eggs to my parents. They'd had the opportunity to visit with the chickens but only during their pre-laying days. With the decision made to deliver them some eggs, the question then became how to transport the eggs across state lines via an airplane.

Not wanting to cross TSA, I thought the best course of action would be to pack the eggs in a checked bag. But, as savvy travelers, or rather impatient travelers, neither Chris nor I were in the mood to check bags and wait at baggage claim in New Orleans. More than that, though, I worried that if we sacrificed and packed them in a checked bag, would the eggs be able to withstand the vast changes in temperature and pressure experienced in the cargo hold of a plane. The thought of arriving in New Orleans and unpacking the bag only to find clothes soaked in yolk and white and peppered with shards of shell, quickly moved us to consider Plan B – carrying the eggs on our person.

I was skeptical that in this post-911 era, where toothpaste and shampoo have been criminalized, that this would be successful. I did not want to have half a dozen eggs cause me to be interrogated, arrested, body-cavity searched, or miss my chance at having a plate of crawfish. Therefore, I conducted a thorough search of internet travel resources.

The search yielded mixed results. It seems that some folks have been successful in packing eggs – both fertilized and non-fertilized – in their carry-on baggage. For each of the successes, however, there are an equal number of failures. Luckily, in none of the cases I read about were people arrested for trying to transport eggs. The risk is that the eggs would be confiscated, and probably destroyed (or maybe consumed) by one or more TSA agents.

Chris did not share my apprehension. Using her hyper-analytical brain, she simply stated that the volume of liquid in an egg is less than an ounce, and therefore would easily pass through security as restrictions on liquids do not kick in until the threshold of 3.4 ounces is breached. I still wasn't convinced and was a little bit worried, so I insisted that the eggs be packed into Chris' bag, not mine.

At the airport, we proceeded to the security screening, had our ID's and boarding passes verified, took off our shoes, placed our bags – one carrying a dozen eggs – on the belt, entered and exited the full body scan machine, collected our bags, put our shoes back on, and headed to the gate. It may have been one of the most seamless trips through security I had ever had. I was relieved yet perturbed.

A few months before, Chris and I were introduced to the Ukranian folk art of Pysanky. Pysanky is a technique that uses wax and dyes to create intricately designed eggs. The process begins with a full egg onto which the dyes are applied in a painstaking process which involves applying wax to the surface of the egg using a kiska – a small brass funnel tied to a wooden stick. The dyes are toxic. Due to the permeable nature of an egg's shell, the contents of the egg are rendered inedible, and must be discarded following decoration (I guess the Ukranians had too many eggs on their hands as well). The contents of the egg are removed by creating a small hole in one end, inserting a small straw and blowing. Looking at the egg, you would have no idea that the egg it was empty. That discovery would only be made if the egg was handled – its weight or lack thereof giving it away.

Couldn't, therefore, a person with evil intent do the same thing? Empty out the contents of an egg, and instead of placing it on a counter as a piece of art, refill the egg with a potent mixture of explosive materials? It reasons that to the colorful list of terrorists which includes the underwear and shoe bombers, could be added the egg bomber. How could the TSA be so short-sighted not to think that someone could hatch an idea to put bombs in eggs?

While we will have to see what if anything comes of this disturbing premonition, at this point eggs are legal.

Not only did we have no problem navigating through security, all eggs survived the journey in the overhead compartment safe and snug in an egg carton encased in a Ziploc Bag. You can never be too careful.

Ironically, during our return flight security screening in New Orleans, my bag was flagged for a manual inspection. On the x-ray machine, the agent spotted something unusual and potentially dangerous. It was not the eggs, as they stayed in New Orleans. It was a mason jar filled with an assortment of buttons my mom gave to me for an arts and craft project. The jar was examined, and found to be harmless, and I was allowed to continue to the gate and my flight home where a dozen fresh eggs, laid while we were away, waited to learn their fate.

Breaking Broody

Her hormones were raging. Her body temperature was high. She was anti-social and irritable. She sat all day in the dark laying box. She wasn't eating. She pulled all her breast feathers out. She stopped laying eggs. She clucked non-stop. Ellen had gone broody. Nature had taken over nurture. Her maternal instincts kicked into high gear, and she was determined to hatch chicks. Without a rooster in the flock, however, the desired outcome would need heavenly intervention – and Ellen, though beautiful, was no angel. Instead, I was now about the task of "breaking broody."

Why it happens to some hens and not others is anyone's guess. Every living thing, from the tiniest one-celled organism to the most complicated of beings, is hard-wired to reproduce. Biological success is not measured in diplomas, awards, friendships, compassion, money or good deeds. Biological success is measured by successfully passing on one's genes to the next generation. And then, that really isn't success. True success occurs when those genes make it not one but two generations down the line.

Chickens lay one egg every 22 hours. However, incubation does not begin until there is a clutch, a group of eggs to be incubated at one time. Were incubation to begin when the first egg is laid, it would result in staggered hatching. The hen would have chicks running around while their brothers and sisters were still developing inside their eggs. Delaying incubation, therefore, ensures that all of the eggs hatch at the same time. Mother Nature ain't no fool.

On average, a chicken clutch contains twelve eggs. The size of the clutch has a built-in insurance policy. Not all of the eggs will hatch. Of those that do, not all will survive to adulthood. They may succumb to disease, predation, or cannibalism from others in the flock. It takes upwards of 20 days for a hen to lay a full clutch of eggs. Incubation typically begins when half the clutch has been laid, and continues for 21 days.

During incubation, the hen ceases to lay any additional eggs. All of her time and attention are now focused on the task at hand. Hens must keep the eggs warm and moist. To accomplish this, the hen does not just simply sit on the clutch. She plucks out a patch of breast feathers to expose her skin enabling the transfer of heat to the eggs. The heat combined with the confined space increases the moisture content of the air, thereby helping to keep the eggs hydrated. The nesting box becomes her whole world. She will likely get off the nest once a day for a few minutes to eat, drink, defecate, take a dust bath or exercise. All hens are different, so this ritual could be in the morning or in the evening, and last for a very short period or as long as half an hour.

Brooding hens usually relieve themselves but once a day in a huge and rather stinky elimination event. Some tenacious hens never seem to leave and don't seem to eat enough. The work of incubation is never-ceasing. During the course of the day, the hens constantly maneuver the eggs, turning them regularly to equalize temperature distribution throughout the egg. Twenty-one days later, all of their hard work and commitment pays off as one by one the chicks begin to emerge from the eggs in all of their fluffy glory.

That's the way it is supposed to happen.

If I presented to you two eggs, one fertilized and one not-fertilized, you would be hard pressed to tell the difference – and your brain is the size of a cantaloupe. Ellen's brain is the size of a pinky fingernail. If it is round, and the size of a golf ball, to her, it is an egg. You can't fault her confusion. Eggs are collected daily so as to discourage broody behavior. An egg appears, and then, a few hours later it is gone. The hen continues to lay, attempting to create a large enough clutch for which to expend the energy necessary to hatch the eggs. No eggs, no clutch.

In our set-up, there is but one laying box that all four hens share. Eggs are usually collected at the end of the day during the evening forage session. This means that at some point during the day, inside the laying box will be a collection of anywhere from one to four eggs. Were Ellen, or any of the other hens to enter the laying box and discover a growing clutch of eggs, it is easy to see how such a sight could trigger the maternal switch.

While the presence of eggs in the coop was a plausible explanation for Ellen's predicament, there is no way to know for sure exactly what turned Ellen broody. Hens have also been known to incubate invisible eggs, and Ellen fell into that camp. Even when the box was devoid of eggs, Ellen eschewed forage time for the laying box. In there, she sits, her body flattened out, incubating nothing but a bunch of hay. However it was triggered, either by the presence of multiple eggs in the laying box, a recent super moon, or voices in her head, the maternal switch was on. The challenge then became how to turn it off.

The key to "breaking broody" is to lower the hen's body temperature. The web was full of suggestions as to how to do this and I systematically worked my way through said suggestions beginning with the most benign which is to remove eggs regularly.

In phase one, instead of waiting until the end of the day to collect eggs, I began to make multiple trips out to the annex to collect eggs as they were laid. The hope was that without eggs, Ellen would be discouraged from brooding. It did not work. Ellen continued to hole herself up in the laying box caring for imaginary eggs.

Phase two built on the efforts of phase one. After removing the eggs, I would then place a handful of ice cubes underneath Ellen. The ice cubes were meant to cool Ellen's body temperature back to its non-broody level. This too failed.

Phase three ramped up the cooling strategy a notch, and added a distraction technique based on an old saying, "madder than a wet hen." In the morning, afternoon and evening, I would take Ellen and immerse her in a tub of water. I was expecting resistance but there was none to be had. Ellen stood very calmly in the tub and seemingly enjoyed, or at least patiently endured, the bath. After approximately five minutes in the tub, I would return Ellen to the flock, either in the annex or out in the yard to forage. The bath seemed to have a positive effect. For a period of time, that between wet chicken and dry chicken, Ellen resumed normal non-broody chicken activities. She ate, she scratched, she remained outside of the laying box, and even stopped clucking. However, once fully dried, Ellen returned to the laying box, assumed the position, and resumed operation incubation.

A still broody Ellen was not only acting to decrease overall egg production but was endangering her own health and well-being. By cock-blocking the laying box and not laying herself, we were down to two eggs, at the most, each day. If not broken soon, Ellen could die from malnutrition. She wasn't eating.

It was time to take more intense measures. Phase four, the isolation chamber, was thus initiated. Experts recommended removing the broody hen from the flock and placing her in a cage raised above the ground, full of food and water, but without any bedding material whatsoever. The raised cage allowed for airflow on all sides of the chicken which acted, as did the ice cubes and water bath, to cool down the hen's internal temperature. The lack of bedding material removed any opportunity to form a nest, a key component of incubation. Separation from the flock separated Ellen from the other's eggs and eliminated, I presume, any other enabling activities that may or may not have been occurring intra-flock.

I set up a wired dog cage outside, just mere feet from and in full sight of the annex. I surmised that, if Ellen were able to see the other three hens fully engaged in normal chicken behavior, it might act to speed up the process of breaking broody. Everything I had read said that two days, three days max would be enough to shut off the maternal switch. It took Ellen a full five days.

After day one of isolation, I let Ellen out to forage with the others. She pecked around the coop anemically for a couple of minutes, then sneaked into the annex and took up residence in the laying box. I tipped over the box, grabbed Ellen, and returned her to the cage. After the third day of isolation, I was hopeful. Ellen pecked more aggressively and stayed with the flock as they scoured the yard. So this time, instead of putting her in the cage, I allowed her to return to the annex. Twenty minutes later, however, when I went to check on her, Ellen was once again in the laying box. It was back to the cage for her.

It bears noting that during Ellen's isolation, egg production from the other hens dropped to one egg a day, and then no eggs. It was a coup de coop. Todd, Nicole and Glynn Anne had organized in protest to Ellen's isolation.

The weather during this breaking broody was quite lovely. It was sunny with temperatures in the seventies. Then the rain came. We had three days of rain. When it rains on the farm, the chickens stay in the coop which they hate. While I was determined to break Ellen, I couldn't see fit to force her into isolation in a cage open to the elements. So, for three days she stayed in the coop waiting out the weather with the other girls, complaining all the while and not laying a single egg.

When the weather broke, and the clouds gave way to sun, I freed all four chickens from confinement. As they reveled, ran, flapped, and scratched, I kept a keen eye on Ellen. She stayed with the flock, pecking with the best of them. It was a good sign, but the real test was yet to come.

After a good long forage session where the population of worms and grubs suffered greatly, I herded the hens into the annex, supplemented their feed with fresh greens and a few burnt biscuits, and waited. At the twenty-minute mark, Ellen was still outside of the laying box. The same was true after one hour, two and three. Ellen was back. Broody had been broken. This was a good thing because phase five would have moved Ellen from the cage to the frying pan whose success rate at breaking broody is 100%.

Crop Block

No longer afflicted with broodiness, Ellen had rejoined the flock and was producing eggs regularly. Then one day in the middle of the evening forage, Ellen stopped in her tracks. Her feathers plumped up, and her backside pulsated. I went in for a closer look. There was something coming out of her cloaca – the exit point for urine, feces, and eggs. It was not an egg, and it didn't look like any chicken poop I had ever seen. It was a long black.

As she continued to flex her muscles, it continued to grow in length, yet it remained attached to her body. When I first noticed her not moving, the thing was approximately 4 inches in length. Over the next 15 minutes, it grew to be 10 inches long and it was obvious that more needed to come out.

I wanted to step in and pull it out myself, but thought better of it. Then at 20 minutes in, Ellen had had enough. Executing an advanced yoga move, Ellen stretched her head between her legs, grabbed hold of the end and pulled. Once free of the encumbrance, she rejoined the flock. Once the encumbrance was free from Ellen, I was able to take an even closer look.

Using two wood chips, I carefully picked it up from the grass and placed it on the deck for dissection. A flimsy black colored membrane encased a vertical mass of undigested grass. For some reason, this was a relief. Ellen hadn't expelled a portion of her intestines, nor had she ingested anything bizarre. It was simply grass - undigested grass.

Chickens don't have teeth. They use their beaks to tear up pieces of grass, pick up feed pellets, insects, worms, and in the case of my chickens, mice. Chickens do have a tongue. The tongue helps push the pieces of food down the throat into the esophagus. As in humans, salivary glands in the mouth excrete saliva which contains water and enzymes to help swallowing and begin the digestive process. Unlike humans, once in the esophagus, food is temporarily stored in a small pouch called the crop. Very little to no digestion occurs in the crop. It is an evolutionary tool designed to allow birds that are hunted by predators to consume large amounts of food in the open then retreat to a safer location to digest.

From the crop, food then passes into the proventriculus or true stomach. It is here where gastric juices like hydrochloric acid begin digestion. The food has yet to be ground up. That takes place in the gizzard, another body structure unique to birds. The gizzard is made up of two sets of stomach muscles which act as the bird's teeth. The contraction of these muscles in conjunction with small stones that birds eat, work to break the food down allowing digestive acids to effectively extract nutrients. Then the process becomes quite mundane. The food passes through the small and then large intestines to the cecum and out through the cloaca or vent. Normal feces produced by chickens is dark in color with a crust of white uric acid crystals. Ellen's poop was not normal. She was not digesting, and it was Chris' fault.

Free ranging chickens, like ours, eat commercial food supplemented by anything and everything they can fit into their mouths. Chickens evolved in the wild. When eating wild food, they usually use their beaks to snip off bite sized pieces of grass and tear off small pieces of insects. These are manageable sized pieces designed to pass easily through the crop into the gizzard. Evolution, did not take into consideration, or hasn't up until this point, lawn mowers.

Spring came on very wet and very hot − great for anything that relies on photosynthesis for growth. Chris and I had already enjoyed many gifts from the garden. But every silver lining has its dark cloud. Along with radishes, asparagus, leeks, and strawberries, we had an overabundance of grass. Chris was cutting the lawn weekly and we were still a full month away from the official start of summer.

Every swipe of the mower left piles of grass clippings 4-6 inches in length depending on the duration between cuts. When the chickens were let out to free range after a cutting, they were met by an all-you-can-eat buffet requiring no tearing. If enough long pieces of grass are piled on top of each other in the crop, it can cause a blockage. This is what we think happened to Ellen. That and maybe a lack of grit, the small pieces of rock that work in the gizzard to break down food.

Crop blockage is serious.

Comparing Ellen's chest to the others, there was a noticeable bulge, the telltale sign of crop block. In advanced cases, surgery is an option. Thankfully, our chickens cannot read. Because serious or not, surgery was not going to be an option – unless quartering a chicken for frying is considered surgery. Instead we opted for a crop massage which I learned about from a YouTube video that detailed the process. How did people ever raise chickens before the internet?

To effectively massage a crop, the chicken must be upside down. Unfortunately, the video tutorial begins with the afflicted chicken already in the upside-down position. I was left on my own to figure out how to flip a chicken.

It was difficult to get Ellen to do anything. This was no exception.

I grabbed her feet. She flapped frenetically. I let go. Round one went to Ellen. I picked her up in one arm, then grabbed the feet with the other, and tried to twist her into position. She flapped, pecked, squawked and moved her body opposite of the intended direction. Round two went to Ellen. I grabbed her feet even more tightly, swung my arm up quickly, and before either of us knew it,

Ellen was subdued, hanging upside down, not struggling, not say-ing a word, resigned. It wasn't a pleasant position for either of us. I'm sure a lot more not pleasant for Ellen than myself. But I wasn't comfortable with her resignation. I could deal with her putting up a good fight. Complete submission was a strange bird.

Once we were both in position, I took my right hand and began feeling around Ellen's neck to find the crop. It wasn't diffi-cult to locate. It was a bulging mass above her breasts. With crop located, I began to gently massage. I can't rightfully say that she enjoyed it, but Ellen did not protest.

In the video, the afflicted chicken regurgitated yellow liquid. Ellen did not regurgitate anything. But when I placed her back inside the coop, the area that was before a bulging mass, was no longer bulging and mirrored that of her coop mates. Of course, for the next few days, morning and night, I paid especially close attention to Ellen's poop. All seemed back to normal. And Chris began running the mower over the grass twice to make the clip-pings smaller and therefore less likely to get tangled in anyone's crop.

Bad Eggs

Soft-Laid Eggs

Chris's cousins were in town visiting for a night and we were all outside engaging in the obligatory chicken experience. The chickens were out and about scratching, dirt bathing and foraging. The humans were out and about sipping cocktails. In the midst of answering one of the many chicken questions asked, I noticed that Todd was no longer ruling the roost that is the dirt bath. Todd was not only fastidious about dirt bathing, being the first in and the last out, but she also was quite territorial about the bath, often pecking and pushing the others out of her way.

My head was always on a swivel when we were outside with the chickens, so I was able to quickly locate the errant bird. She was standing by herself in a patch of grass. A few seconds passed, and she did not move. A few seconds more ticked by and still no movement. Todd stood her ground even when I began to walk towards her. Was she lost in a daydream? Was she engaged in meditation? No. What she was doing was laying an egg.

It was after five in the afternoon. All of the girls were usually finished laying by noon. The timing was way off and so too was the location. Todd had just laid right out in the open, not under the sheltering bushes or in the security of the laying box. After depositing the egg onto the grass, Todd was once again up and moving. All seemed right with the world again. Except that it wasn't.

Upon closer examination, the egg Todd laid was different from all the rest. First, it was taupe in color. As an Easter Egger, Todd laid blue eggs. And the color of a chicken's eggs does not change over time or with any changes in diet or other environmental factors. But more disturbing than the color, was the fact that this egg had no shell. In place of a shell was a soft and squishy leather-like membrane encasing the yolk and egg white.

Months before, Chris's mom had relayed a story about her mother, who grew up on a farm and swore (wrongly) that freshly laid eggs arrived into the world slightly soft and then hardened up within the first minute. Sort of like a baby's skull. We waited for Todd's egg to harden. It did not. Intrigued, we collected the egg and placed it in a bowl on the kitchen counter. We wanted to see how time affected the egg. Over the course of two days, the egg never hardened. It did, however, begin to desiccate, the water content of the egg evaporating into the ether, and the leathery membrane wrinkling.

At this point in my chicken rearing, it came as no surprise that when I beseeched Google with, "Help. My chicken just laid a soft egg," I received thousands of responses. Although the soft egg occurrence is a seemingly common one, the answers as to why, were severely lacking. It could be a lack of calcium, and/or vitamin D which aids in calcium absorption. It could also be related to a change in ambient temperature, a recent stress or loud noise. The search results were inconclusive. Because egg shells are made from calcium, I decided to go with that theory. I upped the amount of oyster shells we mixed into the daily feed rations and provided all the girls, but especially Todd, extra helpings of yogurt before bedtime. After a couple of days, Todd's eggs were back to normal.

Bloody Egg

The third chicken to one day suddenly stop moving, was Glynn Ann. Ironically, it happened while the human Glynn Ann was in Baltimore.

There we were, standing in the backyard going over do's and don'ts when I noticed chicken Glynn Ann standing still. My mounting experience with still chickens told me to wait. She didn't lay a soft-shell egg. I approached and as with the other two instances, she doesn't move. I moved around to her backside hoping to see something hanging out of her back end a la Ellen. There was something on her backside, but it wasn't undigested grass. This time it was blood. The blood was not oozing out of her. It was more or less caked to the feathers forming the perimeter of the cloaca.

She was very docile, not running or walking away from me. I approached and tentatively surveyed the situation. Because there was no active bleeding, I let her alone and looked around for clues. Inside the annex, I found a rogue egg, laid not in the laying box, but in the corner of the annex right on top of the ground devoid of any nest. When I picked it up, the egg was smeared with dirt as well as dried blood. After dozens and dozens of eggs, this was a first. But not a good first like a first kiss or first pay check but more like the first time you have to pick your own blue crab or get your first colonoscopy.

It was getting late. I put Glynn Ann up with the other hens in the coop. I didn't sleep well that night thinking about Glynn Ann (the chicken, not the human). Waking early, I hopped onto the internet to see what could have caused the blood. A unifying theme throughout the posts was cannibalism. Not that cannibalism was the cause of the initial blood, but the fact that chickens cannot help themselves once there is blood. At the sight of blood, chickens will go after each other relentlessly.

Online advice in these cases always involves removing the afflicted hen from the flock. I had done the opposite. I put a bloody hen right in with the others. Based on the information I read, Glynn Ann stood a 50-50 chance of being alive or dead. If she was dead, it was because the other hens had pecked at her bloody vent eventually disemboweling her. Not on any top ten list of ways to die.

I ran out to the coop. All four hens were alive and well.

As with the case of the soft egg, research proved inconclusive. The bloody vent and egg could have been caused by any number of things including mites, busted blood vessel, being egg bound, trying to lay a soft egg, or prolapsed vent (when the pressure of trying to push out a larger than normal egg causes the oviduct to turn inside out and protrude from the vent). None of the causes were reassuring.

When Glynn Ann did finally wake that morning, and the chickens were set free, Glynn Ann the chicken had no new blood, and showed no signs of lethargy. She ambled around the yard with the best of them. Problem solved? For the moment yes. Is that the end of the story? No.

Chicken Chickens

Fear of chickens is called alektorophobia, from the Greek word alektoro meaning rooster, and phobia meaning fear. Surprisingly common, but not widely discussed (at least in polite company), those afflicted with alektorophobia suffer from any combination of nausea, heart palpitations, breathlessness, excessive sweating, shaking, dizziness, dry mouth, the inability to think clearly, or simple madness when coming into contact with or thinking about chickens, living or dead, real or animated. Symptoms can also be triggered by the presence of or thoughts about eggs and feathers.

Alektorophobes believe that, far from being benign, chickens are conspiring against them, coordinating their efforts to exact the greatest degree of injury. Onset of the phobia is often linked to a trauma. The resulting fear is a protection mechanism initiated by the mind. For example, Mickey Rourke's character, Harry Angel in the movie, "Angel Heart," states on several occasions that he has "a thing about chickens" and even refuses an egg. Later on, in the movie, it is disclosed that chickens played a primary role in a satanic ritual Harry witnessed and was trying to block.

Fear can be good, and fear can be bad. It all depends on the type of fear. Rational fear is hardwired into our brains to work with our fight or flight instinct to keep us safe and alive. It can be a good fear. The fear of chickens is an irrational fear and irrational fear serves no beneficial purpose. On the contrary, irrational fear can be detrimental. Given the prevalence of chicken on menus, chicken-centric restaurants, a whole holiday dominated by eggs, and the back section of most grocery stores, trying to live a chickenless life is nearly impossible.

Rational fear is not unique to humans. The fight or flight mechanism is something shared by all animals, including chickens. Loud noises, the call of a hawk, a strange rustle in the bushes all cause the girls' heads to pop up from the feeding position. But are chickens also at risk for developing irrational fears?

It was summer. Heat waves blanketed most of the country. Temperatures were regularly hitting the triple digits; if not hitting them outright, the combination of heat and humidity made it feel like they were. Municipal cooling centers were open, and on the news, folks were encouraged to stay inside.

When Chris and I began our chicken adventure, the first step was matching the right breed of chicken to our personalities as well as to the climatological tendencies of our geography – Central Maryland. It was important to select chickens that could endure the wide range of temperatures experienced in the mid-Atlantic region. While we were careful with our selection, no animal is fully prepared for day upon day of oppressive heat. So when the temperatures began to rise, I began to worry.

I thus made sure that water supplies were more than adequate, and that the annex was positioned to take advantage of maximum shade throughout the day. However, as I sat in the comfort of conditioned air, I worried that the girls might succumb to heat stroke. Chickens do not sweat. They remove excess heat from their bodies through their beaks, often dipping their beaks into water as a way to accelerate cooling. Therefore, in addition to water and shade, I would on occasion bring out to the annex bowls full of ice cubes, hoping that by pecking on the ice cubes, they would be able to better cool themselves. Despite multiple attempts, however, they were no less interested in the ice than playing a game of scrabble.

Although they seemed to be weathering the weather well, albeit with a decrease in egg production, I was still concerned. At about 2 p.m., the hottest part of the day, the protective shade of the yard's foliage gave way to the full fury of the sun's energy. Looking around the yard, I thought there had to be a way to relieve some of the heat. Then I saw it, a large picnic-sized umbrella folded up neatly in a corner.

If I could figure a way to position the umbrella near the annex, the outstretched canvas could provide some level of relief. I grabbed the umbrella, opened it revealing a large swath of orange fabric, and began walking towards the annex. Almost immediately, the chickens began to squawk and fly madly about the annex throwing themselves at the wire mesh sides with no regard to personal safety.

As I tilted the mammoth umbrella into position, I pleaded with the chickens to calm down, explaining that it was just an umbrella. They would not listen to reason and continued to run around like chickens with their heads cut off. I thought that they would calm down as soon as the umbrella was settled into place and I had left the yard. They did not. Instead they stood as far away from the umbrella, exposing themselves to more direct rays from the sun.

Knowing that shade was in their best interest, I ignored their physiological responses, left the umbrella standing guard and retreated to the comfort of air conditioning. At the end of the day, I went out to facilitate the daily walk about. I had to first remove the umbrella in order to unlock the door to the annex. The movement of the umbrella again elicited mass hysteria inside the annex. I moved quickly to throw the umbrella to the ground and open the door.

The chickens bolted from the annex with unusual velocity and vigor. Instead of staying together and in close proximity to the house, they scattered in four separate directions, trying to get as far away from the offending umbrella as chickenly possible.

I waited for them to regroup and commence the normal evening routine. They did not. After more than a year caring for chickens, I had become quite adept at maintaining control over the flock. This evening, it was as if our flock had been replaced by four other chickens who had never before engaged in foraging in this particular backyard. They ran, hopped, and flew away whenever I approached. They dismissed the 4-foot wooden dowel used to encourage them to go in one direction rather than another. They crawled deep into the bushes and brambles marking the perimeter of the property. Then Ellen hopped onto then over the wood pile into the neighbor's back yard.

Screaming, panicked, with sweat pouring out of every pore, I crashed through bushes trying to force Ellen back into the yard. It took a good 45 minutes to round up the quartet of chickens. My body was bruised and scratched. My voice weakened from shouting. My nerve endings pulsed with adrenaline at the effort. I was so angry, that I sent them to bed without their evening yogurt. I couldn't understand. These were not the chickens I had nurtured from peeps into responsible egg-laying hens. These were demon chickens possessed by an unknown force dedicated to chaos.

With the chickens safely locked in the coop, and a double martini in hand, I began to go over in my mind the events of the day, trying to figure out what, if anything, had caused this weird behavior. And mind you, I wanted it to be something. If it was something, then that something could be fixed. If it were nothing, and this was just a precursor for a new behavior model, then the future of chickens at Eastridge was in jeopardy.

The only thing different was the introduction of the umbrella. How could a simple, innocuous umbrella have exacted such a response from the chickens? What was the connection? After a few more sips of the martini, a theory emerged. Maybe the shadow cast by the umbrella in some way mimicked the overhead shadow of the outstretched wings of a hawk or other raptor. The theory seemed entirely plausible; plausible enough for me to claim that that was indeed the cause of the anxiety.

I put the theory to test the next day. The umbrella stayed folded neatly out of sight from any of the chickens. When I let out the chickens in the morning, they did not scatter to the far ends of the earth, but rather stayed in a close-knit flock exploring and scratching in the main part of the yard. When it was time to go into the annex, they dutifully responded to the herding stick, and entered without any complaint.

The theory was holding, but without pulling out the umbrella again, it really had not been tested. However, I wasn't prepared to terrorize the chickens and in the process potentially lose one or more of them to injury or simply lose them to flight just to prove a point. The umbrella remained and remains to this day safely out of sight and mind from the chickens, and life on the farm returned to normal.

Yet I needed a more definitive answer as to what had happened. And when an answer is needed, one goes to the oracle. I first searched generally for known chicken fears, but as expected, that search yielded information dealing with predator-prey relationships. To get at the heart of the matter, I had to put it all on the line and ask if chickens were afraid of umbrellas. While I did discover that humans suffer from a fear of umbrellas, called anorakphobia, a fear of anoraks and other water repelling gear, not one entry mentioned a connection between chickens and umbrellas. The lack of information did not dispel my theory, since my theory relied on the similarity of the shape of an umbrella with the shape of a raptor's wing.

I finally came across a story posted by a chicken owner that led me to what I believed could provide my answer. It was a rainy day, and the chicken owner put on a new slicker that happened to be the color red. As she approached her coop to feed the chickens, the flock became agitated at the sight of her. As she got closer, the agitation level continued to rise until, like our chickens, they were seized by terror. The rain coat happened to be a new purchase. This was the first time she had worn it at all, let alone worn it in the presence of the chickens. And for some reason, she connected the rain coat with the chicken panic, removed the coat, and the chickens at once calmed.

The color of the umbrella in question happened to be bright safety orange, a color akin to red. The focus of my query then shifted to chickens and the fear of orange. Bingo! While not overwhelming, there were a significant enough number of reports of chickens being afraid of the color orange to form some basis of conclusion to the mystery.

It's not common, certainly not ubiquitous amongst all chickens, and most definitely irrational. It is a condition that is shared by about 250,000 Americans, and is known by the name Chrysophobia or fear of the color orange. And while it still could be true that the chickens mistook the umbrella for a hawk, it is somehow comforting to think that the irrational brain is not relegated solely to humans. And begs the question, are we more like chickens than we think, or are chickens more like us?

Cock of the walk?

In municipalities where backyard chickens are legal, there is usually one caveat. No roosters. The reason being that the most iconic of animal sounds, the cock-a-doodle-do, can be construed by some as a nuisance. Contrary to popular belief, the crowing of a rooster is not relegated to sunrise. While most roosters do greet the breaking of a new day with a loud crow, they also crow throughout the day, and sometimes even at night. Crowing is thought to be a territorial warning, a way to communicate with others in the flock in response to a loud sound or in triumph after successfully mounting a hen.

Despite their best efforts, sometimes hatcheries ship out roosters when only hens were ordered. It's easy to tell the males from the females if the breed is one that is sex-linked, meaning that at birth, the males and the females look completely different. The male chicks may be brown for instance, and the females yellow. For those species that are not sex-linked, it comes down to a very specially trained human to make the call.

Correctly sexing a chick is a very difficult and a highly lucrative profession. Chicken sexers make upwards of $60,000 annually. It's an important component of any hatchery. Egg production facilities are only interested in female chicks. Any males born in such operations are separated out and immediately disposed of for having no value (since these particular species are not bred for meat production). It could be said that one of the only places where it is advantageous to be born female, is on the farm.

The mass slaughter of male chicks by means of gas, electrocution and even by grinding them up while still alive, is coming under increasing scrutiny and condemnation. Luckily, technology seems to be providing a solution. Scientists have now figured out a way to take a small sample of the egg fluid, a mere few days after the egg is laid, and use DNA testing to determine the chick's sex.

Using this process, the female eggs are incubated and hatched, and the male eggs redirected to the egg market. So confident are they in the technology, that the United Egg Producers have committed to stop all chick grinding by 2020, a move that will also eliminate all chicken sexing jobs.

Our girls were just fine living on their own with their human roosters who kept them safe and well fed. All of their feathers were intact, which is something their sisters who lived with roosters couldn't say. Roosters tend to tear off hen back feathers during mounting.

That is why it came as such a surprise when the sound of

crowing began emanating from the flock. When it first happened, I frankly couldn't believe my ears. Then it came again and
again. There was no mistaking it. It was a cock-eyed version of
cock-a-doodle-do.

It didn't take long to find the source. There she was – Todd –
standing at attention, craning her neck upwards, beak wide open
crowing, not clucking.

Shakespeare pondered "what's in a name?" I pondered, would
a hen by any other name become a rooster? Todd was the only one
of the girls given a boy's name. Had this innocent gesture caused
major psychological damage?

The answer, according to science, was no.

Apparently, there is some gender fluidity within chickens. It is
not common, but it is also not rare. In all flocks, a normal pecking
order is established early on. In all female flocks, the top bird may
begin to exhibit male characteristics in order to become protector.
In some cases, it is just a weird crow. In others, the hens may cease
laying eggs, develop rooster-like plumage, spurs, and begin mounting the other hens.

In some hens, the change is not prompted by the lack of a
rooster, but by damage done to the left ovary. Birds are born with
two ovaries but utilize only the left one to produce eggs. The right
one lays dormant. However, when the right ovary is damaged, it
causes the left ovary to begin producing testosterone, resulting in
the development of male physiological and behavioral characteristics. Even with the scientific explanation, it is an unusual phenome-
non especially when it is happening to one of your hens.

When this happened in the 1400's, before known scientific
explanation, it was considered witchcraft. In the famous case of the
"Rooster of Basel" in 1474, a hen, that most probably had a damaged left ovary, developed from the very start looking like a rooster.
It had the plumage, the spur, and the signature crow. Unfortunately,

at some point in time, the left ovary must have recovered and the rooster began to lay eggs. Outraged, the clergy took the bird to court where he/she was found guilty and was burned as a witch then cut open to reveal three more eggs lying in wait.

By the 1920's, the climate had become more tolerant of these transgendered chickens. There was a case of a buff Orrington in Britain and the "Rooster of Madison" here in the United States. Both were spared the fate of their sister, the "Rooster of Basel" and lived pretty idyllic chicken lives being regarded simply as curiosities.

Todd wasn't a curiosity. She was part of a modern family, progressive in their thoughts and beliefs. If Todd needed to express herself as a male, that was perfectly fine with me and Chris.

Whether or not she tired of the exercise, or Nicole, Ellen and Glynn Ann put the kybosh on Todd's antics, Todd's crowing soon ceased and the "natural" order of the flock with four hens and two human roosters was restored.

NOTE: Backyard chickeneers are nothing if not resourceful. Wanting roosters in her flock without annoying the neighbors or breaking the law, one backyard chicken farmer invented and patented a collar designed to dramatically reduce both the volume and the frequency of crowing – the No-Crow Rooster Collar. It is not a shock collar like those used for barking dogs. Instead it prevents the full content of the air sac to be expelled all at once, thus muffling the crow. It is made in America and even comes with an optional bowtie.

Something to Crow About

Every four years, the world comes together to do battle on the field, in the pool, around the track, with uneven bars, basket, soccer, and volley balls, javelins, shot puts, and discus, using their hands, their feet, their heart and their might all in pursuit of one of three metal medals. 2012 was one of those years. The location was London. The games, the Summer Olympics.

The battles waged for two weeks and were played out in all their glory and disappointment on TV and the internet. Viewers watched in rapt awe as athletes pushed themselves to run faster and jump higher than they or anyone else had done before. Some succeeded and won. Others fell short, and lost. And each night, at the end of the broadcast or printed on the first page of the morning newspaper was a listing of the medal count by country. China and the U.S. went back and forth all throughout the games. If one was in the lead with total medals, the other would lead in total number of gold medals. In the end, for these games, the U.S. finished in first place in both categories.

But on this greatest stage of sport, the Olympic Creed, adopted in 1908, diminishes the role of the winner while elevating the role of the loser by stating: "The most important thing in the Olympic Games is not to win but to take part, just as the most important thing in life is not the triumph but the struggle. The essential thing is not to have conquered but to have fought well."

It's a confusing notion and one that is also played out during awards shows such as the Emmy's and Oscars when actors state before the ceremonies that winning doesn't really matter. It is the honor just to be nominated. But as Vince Lombardi queried, "If winning isn't everything, then why do they keep score?" Why have different colored medals? Why have any medals at all?

The Olympics may come only once every four years, but the State Fair is an annual event. In Maryland, the State Fair is held at the Timonium Fair Grounds, a mere half mile from our home. Like the forty-nine other state fairs annually held, it is a celebration of all that is agricultural, a vestige of when more Americans were engaged in the agricultural arts than is currently the case. There is also the midway full of rides, fried food and games where one can win giant stuffed animals.

While the majority of fair goers go to stuff their faces and unburden their wallets, the true essence of the fair lies in competition. The scope and range of categories include livestock, produce, arts and crafts, cooking, and eggs.

Our eggs had always lived in a vacuum. It was time to put them to the test. To see how they stood up against eggs from all over Maryland. We would enter them into the Small Producer Miscellaneous Egg Category at the fair, which included colored eggs as well as goose and duck eggs. There is a whole separate category for brown eggs which I reasoned, would have much stiffer competition. This meant the pressure fell to Todd and Ellen.

The entry process was completely automated and online. I simply filled out a form, clicked submit, and it was done. It was mid-summer. The fair did not open until the weekend before Labor Day. Judging was scheduled to take place the day before the fair opened, so the winners could be prominently displayed during the festivities for all to see and to admire. I had two months to get the girls in shape.

The guidance was vague, giving new entrants a decided disadvantage to the "eggperts." I was not deterred.

1. Individual eggs within an entry shall be uniform in

size:

    a. Small size, 18-20 ounces

    b. Medium size, 21-23 ounces

    c. Large size, 24-26 ounces

    d. Extra large size, 27-30 ounces

2. All four sizes to compete in same class

3. Disqualifications:

    a. One or more eggs in entry with adhering dirt or prominent stains over $\frac{1}{4}$ shells surface which causes general appearance of entry to be unclean.

    b. Any inedible egg, according to USDA standards, including large meat or blood spots.

    c. Less than the required number of eggs in entry.

4. Container must be plain - no identification.

5. Exhibitor's flock eggs only.

I decided to concentrate on the uniformity of size and the disqualifications, hoping that the other categories of judging would fall into place. In preparation, two months out, an extra helping of yogurt was dispersed to the chickens to help strengthen the shells. On occasion, Chris would spike the yogurt with a handful of crushed oyster shells hoping for even more of a calcium boost (the girls, however, simply ate around the shells, leaving a congealed mess for morning cleanup).

Twenty days out, the collection and selection of eggs commenced. It was the height of summer. Temperatures were boiling, and as a result, production waned. We would perhaps get one or two eggs a day at best. The pool of qualified eggs was going to be limited. About two weeks out, I found the largest egg I personally had ever encountered either at home or from the grocer's. Both Chris and I were excited. Maybe the extra yogurt was helping. But its size was both a blessing and a curse. It was large. An award-winning egg by any standard, but the competition was to be based on the uniformity of the six eggs entered as a group. If we couldn't elicit five other similarly sized eggs, this mammoth would be worthless.

A week out, and no other blue egg, or brown egg for that matter, ever materialized at the size of this special egg. Chris's parents were in town for a visit. Knowing now that the egg would likely not be amongst those that were entered into the competition, we decided to add it to the breakfast meal.

Chris took out a separate bowl. We wanted to weigh the contents of the mammoth egg against the others. She tapped the egg on the marble countertop a couple of times, peeled one half away from the other, and deposited the contents of the single egg into the bowl – then squealed. It was a double yolker.

There was no real way to attribute the egg to either Todd or Ellen. But being a twin himself, I like to think that Todd was the layer even though Todd the human and Todd the hen share only about 60% of genetic make-up.

After breakfast, we asked Chris' mom to pick out the six best eggs of the lot, taking into consideration uniformity in size and shape. Using her suggestions as a guide, over the next few days, Chris and I continued to play around with the selection. At no time, however, did we even think about dragging out a scale to weigh the eggs. Such is the nature of novices.

On the submittal day, I arranged and rearranged the eggs a dozen times or more, trying my best to put myself into the hearts and minds of the judges. Once the final configuration of eggs was been finalized, I washed each one, scrubbing their exteriors clean of any lingering dirt, debris or poop which would otherwise compromise their chances. I gently placed each egg into a space in the carton, secured the carton with two rubber bands, and headed to the fair.

The fair volunteers were seated behind a folding table with sheets of paper listing all of the competitors. They were welcoming and pleasant. I was a nervous wreck as I handed over the six eggs. Before I left, I was given the opportunity to, at the end of the fair, either pick up the eggs, or donate them to a food bank. I opted for the latter hoping that this small act of kindness would somehow influence the judges' decision. I left. There was nothing more I could do. Everything else lay in the hands of the judges.

I had to wait a full two days before the results were released. The wait was interminable. Then I made the call.

"What's your name?"

"Mitchell. Bronwyn Mitchell"

Shuffling of papers...

"Ah yes. Congratulations! You won eighth place."

"Thank you"

Eighth place? Eighth place? Whoever heard of eighth place? If second place is just the first loser as Dale Earnhardt said, then what, by god is eighth place? I will tell you what eighth place is. Eighth place is one place above ninth place. Eighth place receives a ribbon and prize money totaling $3.00. Eighth place is a winner.

I shouted as I hung up the phone. A smile etched its way across my face so deep and so strong that it would be two days before it was erased. I quickly called Chris to share the news. She was as excited as I was. Our chickens were winners. On my way home, I stopped and bought a premier brand of peach flavored yogurt to give to the girls to celebrate their/our win.

That night, the first night of the Fair, we decided to go see our winning eggs. They were housed in a refrigerated unit, and attached to their plain carton was an orange ribbon. It was the most beautiful ribbon I had ever seen. We took pictures. We told strangers. We walked around the fair our heads held high, our chests puffed up – winners. Vince Lombardi was right.

We would have to wait until the end of the fair to get our hands on the judging sheet to know where our eggs excelled and where they needed improvement. At 9:00 a.m. on the day after the fair closed, I was at the gates of the fairgrounds along with a horde of others eager to claim their ribbons and prize money. There on the table set up in front of the now empty refrigerator, laid out in all their glory, were ribbons in all the colors of the rainbow, including one the color of orange (too bad it would scare the girls too much to show it to them) with my name on it.

After signing a receipt, I was handed a check for $3 as well as the detailed score sheet. We lost 1.5 points on uniformity. Uniformity was based on weight, something that the guidance literature failed to fully explain. All eggs, it seems, must be within .25 ounces of each other not to incur any penalties. Condition and shape also caused us to lose another 1.5 points. My mind, already focused on next year, was thinking that I should scrub a little harder to free the eggs from any stains or dirt, and be more vigilant in selection. The heaviest deductions came in the category of interior which is based on the USDA standards of quality for individual eggs. Not only was this category not well explained in the literature, the information provided in the scoring sheet was ambiguous. To better our outcome next year, I was going to have to invest some time and research this mysterious category.

Where we excelled, where no points were deducted was in the category of texture. The final assessment was a score of 74 out of 100 possible points. I went online to determine how far away we were from the next competitor and of course from first place. While the website listed the names of the winners, it did not list the associated point totals. What I do know is that we will have to do better than 74. The gauntlet has been thrown. Next year the blue ribbon.

EE I EE I OH!

An iconic image of the southern Africa landscape is the termite mound. Growing upwards of thirty feet in height, each mound is painstakingly constructed. One by one, termites excavate soil well beneath the tower, form the soil into tiny balls, cover the balls with termite saliva which acts like cement, and then attach the balls to the ones that came before. Then it is back to the depths where another piece of soil will be found, dug, molded, spit upon, and added to the structure. Like icebergs, the above ground pyramid-shaped structures that dot the landscape belie the super structures underneath. In the case of an iceberg, under the water is just more ice. However, underneath a termite mound is a highly organized and efficient farm. The mound making termites of Southern Africa grow fungus. The termites use woody and plant material as a base to grow the fungus which they then consume. The tower structure is not a living quarters. Instead it is comprised of sophisticated tunnels which can be opened and closed to maintain the underground temperature and humidity at levels conducive to the growth of fungus.

In addition to the termites, seven other non-human animals comprise the magnificent eight who are all known to farm their food. Like termites, leaf cutter ants, ambrosia beetles and marsh snails all farm fungus. Unlike their fungus-farming counterparts, the marsh snails farm above ground on the stalks of marsh grass. Fungi will colonize cuts in the stalks of marsh grass. To facilitate the process, the snails use their rough radula to cut grooves into the grass stalks and then fertilize the grooves by defecating into them thereby speeding the growth rate of the fungus. Rounding out the group of eight are three algae farmers; damsel fish, spotted jelly fish and limpets. Last but not least, there are the farming ants that herd aphids.

Damsel fish live in algae rich coral reefs. To reduce grazing pressure, each fish stakes out a territory and defends this territory against invasion by other herbivores. To increase algal growth rates, the damselfish engage in regular pruning. They also weed their gardens, discarding the more unpalatable types of alga. Limpets employ a similar strategy. They locate a rock face suitable for algal growth, clear the area of barnacles and/or other animals, and tend a film of alga that grows nourished by the daytime sunlight. Then they graze on it during the evening hours. The spotted jellyfish grows its algae inside of its body. Always chasing the sun, the jelly-fish positions itself in a way to maximize photosynthesis.

The last of the agriculturally minded animals are the farming ants. There are several species of ants that herd aphids. The ants do not eat the aphids, they milk them. Aphids excrete a sugary hon-eydew that the ants devour. The aphids are trained to withhold the honeydew until stimulated by gentle strokes from the ants. The ants also train the aphids to defecate in way that makes it easier to har-vest the honeydew. They have been known to transport their herd of aphids when they move to a new location, protect the aphids from predators, and even clip their wings to prevent the aphids from flying off.

For a brief time, this list of elite adapters was extended in the most unlikely of ways. In a twist, often referred to as irony, four domesticated chickens being farmed for their eggs, secretly oper-ated an underground agricultural enterprise.

There was a hint of something happening in the coop. A mal-odorous aroma emanated from the coop and began to grow in strength. I smelled it during my daily chicken chores even noting that the smell was gaining in intensity. But farms have a smell. So I chalked up the odor as normal and ignored it. My smell receptors slowly but surely adjusted, moving the smell from the obtrusive to the innocuous category.

Chris, who is the chickens' secondary care giver and as such spends less one-on-four time with them, had a decidedly different take on the smell. While setting up for an outdoor party we were giving, her uncorrupted smell receptors, under an uncontrolled assault, sent an alarm signal from nose to brain saying something was not right. She immediately stopped what she was doing and rushed into the house to ask me, the primary chicken care giver, about the smell.

"That's what a farm smells like," I said. This was, apparently, not the answer Chris was looking or hoping to receive. She turned, muttered something, and left the room – a woman on a mission. Being a woman, I know that it is best to stay out of the way of a woman on a mission. This advice is doubly true when that woman is Chris Pavlick. Therefore, I simply returned to whatever it was that I was doing prior, not giving the smell a second sniff.

Approximately 30 minutes later when the next party related decision had to be made, I went out to find Chris. She was in the backyard, sweating, swearing and swallowing down the contents of her stomach which were trying mightily to escape through her mouth. Single-handedly, Chris had managed to move the coop out into the middle of the yard.

The bottom of the coop is fitted with heavy wire to prevent any predators from reaching the chickens by burrowing underneath. While great at keeping out predators, the wire is, at least from the human perspective, an uncomfortable surface over which to walk. Even with a healthy layer of wood shavings and/or straw, the well-being of the chickens' feet was definitely considered when siting the coop. Chris and I made sure that the bottom of the coop was more than flush with the surface of the earth so as to provide stability and comfort.

Raising chickens is not complicated, and is not cheap. When I saw an ad on Craig's List for free straw, Chris and I jumped. Instead of buying wood shavings for bedding material from the feed store, we used the free straw. After a few months, however, it became obvious that the properties of straw and wood shavings were quite different. The wood shavings absorb more waste and break down more easily than the straw which, when wet, becomes a coagulant mass whose moisture content never evaporates.

Chris decided that the wood shavings would be used in the upper part of the coop; the part where the girls seemed to sleep and oddly enough defecate the most. The straw would be relegated to the bottom half of the coop to serve as a cushioning barrier against the wire cage bottom. This arrangement seemed to work – until the rains came.

There may have been a drought in the middle part of the country, but in the Mid-Atlantic, it was a very wet summer. The rains came often and were often violent in nature accompanied by heavy winds. We even played witness to an obscure weather condition known as a derecho which is basically a horizontal tornado.

The rain kept the contents of the coop in a perpetual state of dampness. To help soak up the water and give the girls a drier footing, I would often just add a layer of new straw on top of the old. Again, this worked for a while. But the non-absorbent nature of the straw just led to a denser mat of semi-decaying cellulose. It wasn't pretty, but the girls seemed to be doing fine. In fact, they began to spend a lot of time in and around the coop even during their morning and evening walk-abouts.

It wasn't until Chris pulled the coop from its home position that we learned the reason for chickens' sudden increased interest in the coop. And the reason for the putrid odor. The combination of rotting, wet straw, chicken poop and warm temperatures had created the perfect breeding ground for maggots.

Underneath the coop to a depth of four inches below ground was a maggot nest – a writhing mass of fly larva. While the chickens may not have initiated the operation, they were no less farming maggots; feeding them with their poop and then harvesting the crop as they emerged from the ground through the openings in the wire mesh.

The sight of the maggots was disturbing. Were their food source not already known, a casual viewer might have called the police to report that a dead body must certainly lay somewhere underneath. The smell, which had been partially contained by layers of straw, now wafted through the air unabated. My nostrils tickled and the hairs on my arms stood at attention.

Always trying to save money, I suggested to Chris that maintaining the maggot farm would cut down on the feed expenditures. She ignored the suggestion and continued to dig, unearthing more and more maggot nests.

She excavated down four to six inches of the maggot laden soil, basically the entire area upon which the coop sat. This spoil material was transported away from the house and deposited out in the forested buffer at the far end of the yard, and with it the smell.

We returned the coop to its former position, filled it completely with sweet smelling wood chips, refilled the water and feed containers and put the chickens up for the night. When they entered the coop, one by one they began to scratch at the floor, anxious to harvest the ripe crop of maggots that they had been so carefully tending. Their scratches yielded nothing but wood chips and wire. Undaunted, they scratched some more. Still their efforts came up empty. They looked confused and agitated. They had spent all day in the annex dreaming about maggots. But the jig was up. They had been found out.

The secret maggot farm was no longer a secret and no longer existed. Their dreams of being added permanently to the list of the magnificent eight animal agriculturists had been forever crushed. Their future looked bleaker than it had just a few hours earlier. For it was back to a diet of pellets and the random cricket or worm scavenged over the course of a day. And to add insult to injury, they were going to be picked up, pestered, and no doubt pinched by a throng of thirty or more party-goers whose only experience with chickens involved a plate, fork and knife.

But the gods must have a soft spot in their hearts for chickens who bravely challenge what it means to be a chicken, who eschew the status quo, who find it more comfortable trail blazing a new path rather than simply following the crowd, who become farmers instead of simply being farmed. For after months of planning, the party scheduled to take place on a nice crisp pre-autumn evening out of doors, the same party that led to the discovery of the maggot farm, was forced inside due to rain. There may be four less farmers living at Eastridge, but the chickens got the last laugh.

Light as a Feather Stiff as a Board

Three Dog Night had it all wrong. One is not the loneliest number – three is. Today we buried Glynn Ann. By the numbers, the flock had been reduced by 25%. But the loss of a family member cannot be measured in numbers. It cuts a hole in the heart which is ineptly filled with memories, could-have-beens, and should-have-beens.

Glynn Ann always marched to the beat of her own drummer. She was always the first out of the coop or annex, and the last hen in. She was frustratingly independent. Never content to eat the grass right in front of her, she always went searching, seeking, for the freshest and greenest sprigs. And when cornered, the other three would assume the crouched position, a position of subservience, Glynn Ann would run, fly, scurry, and peck her way to freedom.

There is one call, however, that no bird, no matter how indomitable in spirit, can escape. When death calls, the answering machine never picks up. That call rings and rings and rings until exhaustion or insanity compels all birds to answer.

I had noticed less pep in Glynn Ann's step than per normal. I had also noticed that the rear feathers flanking her vent were always crusted with feces. These changes were noted and filed. Other than these two minor things, she was still eating, drinking, and refusing to come when called.

Things then took a turn for the worse. Her behind was always caked with residue (the others were clean). And then her bright red comb began to shrink in size and fade from bright red to a pale pink. This is when concern set in.

I scanned the online backyard chicken forums for advice. Others in the same position as I now found myself had posted questions about lethargic hens with pale combs. The advice and guidance was all over the place. But it boiled down to one of two possible scenarios. Either she was about to molt, or she was about to die.

Then one day after arriving home from work and throwing my purse down on top of the dining room table, I walked to the window to check on the girls in their annex. All I saw was a pile of white feathers. Fear took grip. That fox who had been skulking around of late had made its move – and somehow got to Todd.

I ran out the back door certain to find only bits and pieces of chickens. But I found all four safely ensconced in the annex. Todd, it seemed, had begun to molt. Molting usually occurs once a year. It is when a hen loses and re-grows her feathers. Apparently molting has an evolutionary purpose. It is regular maintenance like an oil change for a car, which allows a bird to effectively evade predation.

During a molt, the normal cycling of hormones is disrupted. Growing new feathers takes proteins and energy. The hens' bodies cease producing eggs in order to fuel feather production. It seems that the rate and extent of a molt is directly proportional to a bird's egg producing ability. Poor producing hens molt early, and often stay in an extended state of molt. Whereas, high producing hens molt late and quickly. There is a definite pattern of feather loss that begins with the head then proceeds to the neck, then the breast, thighs, back, wings and finally the tail feathers.

Todd's molt, to date, was the most extensive. Like her name-sake, her head was almost completely devoid of feathers as was her underbelly and tail. Ellen's molt was slow to progress. Nicole's loss was most pronounced on her tail. But she was the only one of the four – make that three – that was still producing. And Glynn Ann, well, Glynn Ann never made it to molt.

With Todd in full molt, both Chris and I held out hope that Glyn Ann's behavior change signaled the impending loss and re-growth of feathers. Yet, as the days progressed, my hope began to wane. Glynn Ann's lethargy increased almost exponentially day by day. She would come out of the annex and coop, walk a few steps, skip a few times to evade my capture, and that was it. I still saw her eating both inside and outside of the coop and I took that as a good sign.

It should be noted that during Glynn Ann's decline, none of the other birds showed any signs of weakening constitution or crusty tail feathers. This, I concluded was a good sign, for whatever it was, it was confined to Glynn Ann and Glynn Ann alone.

Ruling out molting as a cause for her decline, I narrowed down my diagnosis to either cancer or sour crop. Having no way to diagnose chicken cancer, I concentrated on her crop. It was extended. She was evidently not having regular bowel movements. The problem, I deduced, was digestive in nature.

As directed by the oracle, I gave Glynn Ann daily crop massages, hoping to either dislodge a blockage, or at the least, release any pent-up gas. I also gave her a warm bath hoping to dislodge an egg, if one happened to be stuck and at the same time cleaned up her backside. The massage and bath did little good and Glynn Ann's condition continued to worsen.

Chickens cannot vomit on their own. I tried to empty Glynn Ann's crop by holding her upside down. A while back, this technique seemed to help Ellen. Glynn Ann did not put up a fight as I grabbed hold of her legs and moved her body 180 degrees. Neither did she vomit.

More and more certain that Glynn Ann's condition was sour

crop, I searched for more and better remedies. I began to isolate
her during the day so as to give her time and space to heal without
being pushed or stepped upon by the others. I fed her food that had
been soaked in water, yogurt and olive oil to aid in digestion. Again,
she ate, but ate sparingly.

In order to give her more comfort and respite, I decided to
extend her isolation from the other three to overnight. I set up the
cat carrier with a nice bed of fresh wood shavings, and prepared a
nice bowl of mushy food and water. I also decided to induce vom-
iting once more. This time not from an upside-down position, but
from right side up, pushing the contents of her crop up through her
beak. The technique worked. Glynn Ann vomited a good amount
of yellow liquid, which I took as a good sign. Get the poison out.

Perhaps it was the wrong thing to do for in the morning, when
I went down to check on the chickens, there lying still and hard to
the touch was Glynn Ann. She was gone.

I let the other three out for their morning walk about, put
them in the annex for the day and put a call in to Chris who was
in North Carolina visiting her aunt and cousins. When she picked
up the phone, the first words out of my mouth were, "Glynn Ann
is dead."

Removed from the immediate situation, Chris calmly directed
me to wrap Glynn Ann in a garbage bag and put her in the freezer.
We would bury her upon Chris' return.

I didn't immediately run down to the basement. Instead I
made breakfast, watched a little TV – procrastinated. But as the
sun continued its rise into the western sky, warming the day into
the 70's, I knew that the job had to be done sooner rather than later.

Many have asked, why not just eat her? In all honesty, I would
have. I have stood upon many a soap box and preached that if
you eat meat, then you should be able to kill and eat an animal. It
would have been hard, but I would have forced myself to do it, after

a couple of gin martinis as appetizers. However, everything I've read has warned not to eat any bird that has died due to disease. That's not to say I didn't indulge in a gin martini or two that evening. But chicken was what was not for dinner.

I knelt down on the ground and as gently as I could, pulled Glynn Ann from the cat carrier and wrapped her in a plastic bag. Even though she was hard to the touch and her head was tilted at a very unnatural angle, I was terrified of suffocating a potentially alive bird. Maybe I have lived in Baltimore – land of Edgar Allen Poe – for too long.

After putting her into one bag, a tall kitchen bag, I waited and watched for any perceptible movement indicating life. At least partially convinced, I placed the first bag into a second bag, this time, a large, black lawn-style garbage bag. Again, I waited and watched for the bag to move in rhythm to the inhale and exhale of a breath. Again, there was none.

Before moving Glynn Ann, I went to the freezer to make room. Chris freezes large blocks of ice in plastic containers in order to keep the interior temperature of the freezer low. Thereby lessening the amount of electricity needed to keep the freezer cold and saving electricity. The freezer in question is a full-size freezer. I surveyed my space options. On the bottom shelf, a large orange Tupperware container filled with ice, if moved, would make enough room for Glynn Ann.

It wasn't until I had Glynn Ann cradled in my arms ready to be placed in the freezer that I realized that the only other thing on that bottom shelf was a frozen turkey – the free one received for spending a certain amount of money ahead of Thanksgiving. Company? Irony? Bad joke?

I closed and locked the door and then checked three times to make sure that the door was in fact locked before heading upstairs. Chris wasn't due home for another 24 hours. During that time and for another 10 hours after she arrived home, I never once ventured downstairs into the basement. Maybe I had seen one too many horror movies, but I did not want to be the one who opened the freezer door only to be attacked by a very cold and very angry chicken.

I made Chris do it.

And when she opened the door, she was met only by a freezer full of dead animal parts, and on the third shelf, a turkey in shrink-wrapped plastic and a hen encased in two garbage bags.

Chris also dug the grave, in the garden near two other dearly departed pets, cats who died of leukemia. I read that in order to avoid unwanted scavengers, the grave should be dug to a depth of no less than two feet and then covered with large rocks.

To speed decomposition, and thereby rebirth, the two layers of plastic bags were removed. Chris placed Glynn Ann into the grave with her head facing out towards the yard. A few awkward words were said, and a few tears shed, before Glynn Ann's body was covered over with earth and then stone.

Prior to the burial, I let the other three hens out for their afternoon walkabout. This would be the last time the four of them would enjoy the evening sky together. They scratched and pecked, flew and stretched their wings, unaware of the somber occasion. I watched them intently, keeping an eye on their whereabouts, but also to note any semblance of knowing. Either their pinky-nail sized brains did not register the death, or in a final tribute, they chose to do as Glynn Ann would want them to do; not waste one moment on grief but peck and scratch as if there was no tomorrow – because sometimes there isn't. My much larger brain knows it was the former, but I choose to believe the latter.

Rest well Glynn Ann. You were loved, and you are missed.

Not What It's Cracked Up To Be

It may be cute, even inspirational when animated lions sing it, but the circle of life be damned.

What started as an ordinary day turned out to be something altogether not. Give me the ordinary, the mundane, the boring. Give me routine, dull, humdrum. Hell, I will even take tedious. Just turn back the clock and give me back my chickens.

It was a Saturday morning, a lazy Saturday morning. Neither Chris nor I was in any rush to tend to the chickens. The diminished flock had made it through another winter. Even though the calendar read spring, frost was still the flavor of the morning. As I sat, eyes idly perusing a computer, I called out reminders to Chris, "It's your turn to do the chickens," "The chickens don't like to be kept waiting," "Chickens, Chickens, Chickens." Not once did I get up from a seated position and walk over to the window to look out into the yard. I just sat there on a day like the day before, and the day before that, naively assuming that three chickens were awake, pecking at the pellet food but eager to stretch their wings, eat some green grass and surprise an unsuspecting worm or twenty. It was a glorious ordinary day. Until it wasn't.

Chris slipped on her outside shoes and tromped off to free the chickens from their nightly confinement. No sooner had she left when she returned, and the three words no keeper of chickens wants to hear came out of her mouth, "The chickens are gone!"

Gone? Gone where? Gone how? Gone why?

Still in my pajamas, I grabbed a pair of shoes and ran outside. The window door of the coop was open. There were no chickens to be seen in or around the coop. The search was on.

Chris' first thought was that someone stole the chickens. At that point, all theories were viable.

Chris went left, I went right, walking around the side of the house, a place where the chickens liked to forage despite my protestations. My eyes were fixed upwards, thinking that they had taken refuge in the trees, though never had they ever done that. I walked the full length of the house, out to the street, scanning the neighborhood. I saw nothing. On my way back, however, my eyes happened to cast downward for a second and then the reality of the situation took hold. It wasn't someone that took the chickens, it was something. Funny I hadn't seen it on my first pass through, so obvious it was now. There beneath my feet lay a pile of tan and black feathers. The remnants of what once, only a few hours hence, was Ellen.

Shock, dismay, grief took hold and I cried out in a wail enviable of professional mourners hired to attend funerals in developing countries. Though this was no show. It was visceral. It was pain incarnate.

Still wailing, I flopped to the ground, unable to stand. Worried about the neighbors, Chris urged – no demanded – I stand up and calm down.

The search continued. Chris went to the side of the house to confirm my findings. I headed to the end of the property, where I doubted the chickens would have ever ventured, then turned left into the neighbor's yard. I was no longer looking up. My gaze was fixed on the ground. Two steps in, another pile of feathers, another wail. I had found Todd.

The physical properties that govern this physical world fell away. I was spinning, a whirling dervish of grief, unable to stand, unable to form words, unable to comprehend the tragedy that was unfolding. Chris continued the search only after I agreed to go inside the house. The confines of the house were of little comfort. I cried, screamed, crawled around on the floor seeking solace from the cold hard wood planks. Chris continued the search. Hope sprang eternal. Nicole was yet to be found. Could it be she was able to evade the evil predator? Could it be that she was still alive, scared and alone perched on some branch of some tree somewhere in the yard or very near?

Maybe. Yes. Yes. Yes. Yes. No.

Once able to stand upright, I headed once more out into the backyard where I found Chris carrying a cardboard box. The box was only a bit larger than the one, almost two years to the day, I picked up at the post office holding four one-day-old chicks. This box held within it the remnants of all three chickens, Todd, Nicole, and Ellen. My heart officially broke, and I took refuge in bed under the covers. And there I stayed for the next six hours while Chris contemplated calling 911 to have me committed.

The pain of the loss was intolerable. I called my mother that morning even before Nicole had been found. I was sobbing. She was sympathetic. She called back that evening. I was still sobbing. She explained that the official mourning period for the chickens was now over. I needed to dry my eyes and move on. It was her hypothesis that the scope and depth of the sadness was multiplied to this irrational level because in the beginning, Chris and I chose to name the chickens after our friends instead of fictional characters, or other cutesy monikers. Therefore, she reasoned, my mind was confusing the loss of the chickens with the loss of my friends.

While I am cautious to giving any of my mother's hypotheses much credit, I did feel better after speaking on the phone with Todd and Nicole, the humans. I think it had more to do with the associated sympathy than a reassurance of their current state of being alive rather than dead.

I tried to quell the tears, to staunch the sobs, to turn off the images in my head, but I couldn't. Not even an extra-large martini seemed to help.

What had happened? I went over the details of the previous evening with a fine-toothed comb. The sun was out, and while not warm, it wasn't cold. Chris and I had both been in the back yard trying to figure out the best location for our newest endeavor – bee-keeping. The girls scratched the ground and even had time for a nice long dust bath before they were rounded up for the night. Chris and I had plans. We were off to the city for a date night. All three went into the coop with little protestation even without yogurt. All of the latches were secured as they had been secured for nearly the last 700 nights. But that morning, the coop was open and empty.

Chris had done some sleuthing but there was no sign of forced entry. There were no tell-tale signs, no scratch marks, no busted wires, no earth was disturbed. How the fox gained ingress remains a mystery. Pecking at the back of my brain was the thought that will drive me mad if I let it but will surely haunt all the rest of my days. Was human error to blame? Did either Chris or I fail to properly secure one or more of the latches?

Chickens are deep sleepers. Forget about sleeping like a baby. What you really want is the ability to sleep like a chicken. On those rare occasions, when night fell before the chickens were herded into the coop, they would perch on top of the roosting box and fall asleep. One by one, I would pick each up, still asleep, and deposit them into the coop.

Is that what happened? Did the fox simply grab each out from the coop, reversing the process, dispatching with one before return-ing for another? Or did adrenaline production kick into high gear and three epic chases ensue with only one outcome? I like to think the latter – that the girls at least made the fox work for his or her meal. That it was an epic battle the likes of which would make David Attenborough proud.

All winter long, the nights had been quiet. No sight or sound of fox to be had. About a month before the night that changed everything, Chris roused me from bed. The woods were alive with the sound of foxes which sound more like a human baby being strangled than anything else – though I have never heard a baby being strangled. It is a scary sound, a dangerous sound, a haunting sound.

Looking back, perhaps it was the sound of a fox in labor. By the calendar it was spring and the time of new birth. By the thermometer, it was still winter. Maybe climate chaos had something to do with this. For at this point in the calendar year, rabbits and mice and squirrels and insects, the foodstuffs of the fox should be out and about in high supply. There shouldn't have been a need for the fox to come into a mowed lawn only 20 feet from human habitation looking for a meal. But something compelled the fox to enter the domain of its own personal predator – man. That something had to be hunger. Hunger felt not only by itself but also by its kits, its progeny, its lifeline to genetic immortality.

The fox had no more choice than a drowning man has of trying to take a breath under water. As a scientist I understand this. As the "mother" of chickens, that explanation falls upon deaf ears. My anger towards the fox only grew when at 3 o'clock in the morning – most probably 24 hours since its last meal – I saw him back in the yard nosing around the coop looking for more.

I was unable to sleep. Each time I closed my eyes, images of Todd, Nicole, and Ellen played across my eyelids. I got up, got a drink of water, and for some reason turned on the backyard light. This happened three nights in a row. Each time I turned on the light, there was the fox. On the fourth night, no fox. Had he finally given up or were the three visits symbolic of the three chickens.

When tragedy strikes, you look for symbols everywhere.

There is no gun in the house. If there were, the fox was in no real danger. All I could do was watch and cry.

Sure, I wanted to exact revenge, but to what end? The chickens were gone. But I am from Louisiana whose capitol city is Baton Rouge, so named because Indians bled out kills on sticks as a warning to others. I could make an example of that fox, and to any other fox that dared to come near. I could drape a fox stole round my neck each time I ventured into the backyard or stake up a fox kin at the border between the backyard and the wooded perimeter as a warning. These thoughts crossed my mind and provided a bit of comfort.

Comfort also came in the form of condolence messages. On Sunday morning, 48 hours after the loss, I mustered enough energy to change my Facebook photo to one that featured me holding all four chickens. And I announced to the world in my status that the chickens were dead. This announcement was echoed on the Baltimore County Chicken Revolution Facebook page, and individual emails were sent to friends who eschew Facebook altogether.

The responses were quick, heavy and heartfelt. The most comforting, in a macabre way, was one from a fellow church parishioner who said that her dog had caught and dispatched a fox that same night.

And right about then, my new employer, The Maryland Agricultural Resource Council decided to host the first of four films in its Farm Fresh Flicks: A Seedy Collection of Films. In addition to the film screening of "Mad City Chickens" – an homage to the backyard chicken keeper – there was a panel of chicken experts on hand to answer any and all questions regarding chickens so I was eager to attend.

During the Q & A, I asked if the rise in backyard chicken keepers was being met with a similar rise in the number of veterinarians qualified to diagnose and cure chickens. The answer was no. This I knew too well from when Glynn Ann succumbed to what I diagnosed as sour crop, and vet after vet I called could offer no guidance. The conversation then moved on to address the average laying lives of hens and their ultimate endings.

The experts were in agreement – as I already knew – a hen is good for laying for approximately two years. Chris and I had briefly discussed what to do when the chickens stopped laying completely, as their life expectancy far outweighed that time period. We joked about sending them to the country – to a rest home – while the reality of having to kill and eat them floated around the rational parts of our brain. It was hard to eat that first egg. It would have been harder still to have to process the girls for personal use. Luckily, we didn't have to make that final decision. That decision was made for us.

I like to think we would have had the guts to wring their necks, pluck their feathers, and create three meals worthy of royalty. However, I don't have that luxury or burden. Right now, all we have are four feathers one from each girl (we kept one from poor Glynn Ann), five eggs, a hole in the heart, and an empty coop.

Though short-lived, those chickens lived well. Though small in stature, those chickens were a giant part of our lives. Though each day the hawk flew overhead, and the fox stalked the night, those chickens lived in the moment unburdened by the stress of what may happen, what could happen. Though gone, those chickens are not forgotten.

Epilogue

Chris is ready to begin anew, to order a new flock. She is also researching a variety of anti-fox technologies to employ to ensure something like this never happens again. There are many varieties of electrified fencing, heavy duty locks, smell deterrents, and even a motion detection camera affixed to a sprinkler.

I'm not quite there yet. The coop and the annex still stand empty. I have a hard time looking out the window to the backyard let alone going into the backyard, still holding out hope that this is all some sort of nightmare, a cheap ploy to finish this book. Still hoping beyond hope that Todd, Nicole, Ellen, and for that matter Glynn Ann will be craning their necks at the sound of the back door opening, waiting to be let out for a walk about.

After the emotional toil the loss of the girls caused, the thought of a second flock is the furthest thing from my mind. My chicken days are behind me. It is time to move on to something new. I signed up for an Introduction to Beekeeping class. With 15-30,0000 bees in a hive at any one time, it is unlikely I will get emotionally attached to any particular bee or bees.

Chris, however, is of a different mindset. She put in an order for six chicks and is designing a new coop. I respond with indifference. If she wants chickens, she should have chickens. These will be her chickens. I will be hands off. Chris agrees enthusiastically.

The six arrive and are named, not for friends but by friends. The old coop is sold, and a new coop built. The chicks grow into pullets then hens, and begin to produce eggs. That is perhaps where the similarity with flock #1 ends. These are definitely second-flock chickens and we are second-flock parents.

Given our hard-earned experience, our over-protective, heli-coptering, constant state-of-worry days are over. Chickens are a strong and resilient lot. With food, water, shelter, and space, they manage quite well – with or without humans. Luckily, they can tolerate living with us – and our lives are the better for it.

The Last Word on Chickens

One only needs to look to the English language to know that the bonds between humans and chickens run long and deep. Since embarking on our life with chickens, some of these expressions have much more meaning for us. Some remain a mystery. All, however, speak to inextricable bond between chicken and man that no law can put asunder. This is just a small sample.

- Flew the coop – Up and left home.

- Up with the chickens – Early riser.

- Henpecked – For a woman to consistently criticize and bully a male – namely a husband.

- Nobody here but us chickens – This saying is often used as a prelude to a secret. Go ahead, talk, no one is around to hear. NOTE: Chickens are good listeners and cost much less than a traditional therapist.

- Madder than a wet hen – As our chickens have yet to be rained upon or bathed, I am unable to authenticate this saying.

- Do chickens have lips – Kin to "Does a bear poop in the woods" is the answer to a stupid question. I can attest that chickens do not have lips.

- Don't count your chickens before they hatch – On average 20%

of a given clutch of eggs will not hatch. In addition, a variety of predators seem to enjoy supplementing their diets with fresh eggs.

- Hen party – This is the female equivalent of a stag party.

- Like a chicken with its head cut off – To act in a haphazard or aimless way; to act frantically or without control. When a chicken, or for that matter – a human – has its head cut off the body will twitch and flail about for a while. This is commonly attributed to post-mortem neural transmissions. However, due to their physiology, a chicken can have its head cut off and remain living. This happens if the cut is too high leaving a portion of the brain and missing the jugular vein. This happened in 1945 with "Miracle Mike". Mike survived decapitation – and was then fed with an eyedropper for a year until he choked on a kernel of corn.

- Like a head with its chicken cut off – depressed

- You can kiss a chicken's XXXX but you won't get any more eggs (than you get now)..." – This saying is used to illustrate the futility of brown-nosing to get ahead.

- I'll be on you like a 'banty' on a june bug – Chickens are omnivores. Insects beware!

- Don't ruffle my feathers – To annoy or irritate another.

- I'm broody, go away – A sour disposition. Chickens brood when they are incubating a clutch of eggs. She leaves the nest once daily to eat and poop. She guards the clutch – not letting any other chicken come close.

- A whistling woman and a crowing hen always come to some bad end! AND A whistling woman and cacklin' hen, ain't fit for garden or men. – HUH????

- The cock may crow but it's the hen who lays an egg – While the male struts about making a lot of noise – it is the female that gets the work accomplished.

- Aaplicar la ley del galllinero. - Spanish - 'apply the law of the henhouse' meaning a hen which sits on top soils the ones below.

- As happy as a rooster in a hen house – Self-explanatory.

- I feel cooped up – Feeling boxed in.

- Fussing like an old hen - Angry

- Scratching out a living. – To get by on very few resources. Chickens spend the entire day scratching at the ground to uncover seeds and insects.

- Work as hard as a hen hauling wood – This means hardworking. Our chickens are layers. Perhaps there is a variety that works in the forestry industry?

- Rulin' the roost – Be the boss.

- Chick - Commonly used to refer to a young woman.

- Don't cackle if you haven't laid – don't complain if you haven't finished your part of the effort.

- Pecking order – finding your place.

- Chicken feed – Not a lot of money.

- Which came first the chicken or the egg? – Only God knows.

- Curses are like chickens; they always come home to roost. - Your offensive words or actions are likely at some point to rebound on you.

- Don't put all your eggs in one basket. AND Don't spend the egg money before the hen lays the eggs. Don't plan on an outcome before it actually happens.

- Chicken scratch - Meaning bad handwriting. While none of the chickens have asked for a pencil and paper, the configuration of a chicken foot seems incompatible with writing.

- To lay an egg - Meaning to fail, this saying is a bit ironic because success in this case literally means laying an egg.

- All chickens are the same color in the dark – Aren't we all?

- Long long ago, when chickens had teeth - Instead of "Once upon a time…

- Playing chicken – The game in which the loser is the one who jumps out of the way first.

- "Why don't chickens pee, they drink water?" - This is used to answer a question when one just doesn't know the answer. Chickens, like all birds pee and poop in one – very efficient.

- Out there where the hoot owls 'get friendly' with the chickens. – This means a really remote location because an owl will eat a chicken just as fast as a college student on 35 cent wing night.

- That's like puttin' socks on a banty rooster. - Something hard to do.

- The turtle lays thousands of eggs without anyone knowing, but when the hen lays an egg, the whole country is informed. - Malaysian Proverb

- If you were born lucky, even your rooster will lay eggs. - Russian Proverb

- Even a blind hen sometimes finds a grain. - German proverb

- "Grasshopper always wrong in argument with chicken." - Book of Chan

Quotable Chicken Quotes

- "A hen is only an egg's way of making another egg." - Samuel Butler

- "I want there to be no peasant in my kingdom so poor that he cannot have a chicken in his pot every Sunday" - Henry IV

- "The key to everything is patience. You get the chicken by hatching the egg, not by smashing it." – unknown

- "Chicken one day, feathers the next" – unknown

- "We can see a thousand miracles around us every day. What is more supernatural than an egg yolk turning into a chicken?" - S. Parkes Cadman

- "Business is never so healthy as when, like a chicken, it must do a certain amount of scratching for what it gets" - Henry Ford

- "Sticking feathers up your butt does not make you a chicken." - Chuck Palahniuk

- "Religion is no more the parent of morality than an incubator is the mother of a chicken." - Lemuel K. Washburn

- "I'll change you from a rooster to a hen with one shot!" Dolly Parton's character in 9 to 5 movie

- "Regard it as just as desirable to build a chicken house as to build a cathedral." - Frank Lloyd Wright

- "Love, like a chicken salad a restaurant has, must be taken with blind faith or it loses its flavor" - Helen Rowland

- "It is better to be the head of chicken than the rear end of an ox" - Japanese Proverb quotes

- "Ain't nobody here but us chickens" - Song lyrics, Louis Jordan

- "The Sky is falling!" - Chicken Little, children's fable

- "Boys, I may not know much, but I know chicken poop from chicken salad." - Lyndon B. Johnson

- "The difference between 'involvement' and 'commitment' is like an eggs-and-ham breakfast: the chicken was 'involved' - the pig was 'committed'."

- "A chicken in every pot" - 1928 Republican Party campaign slogan

- "Don't have a pot to put it in" - 1928 Democratic Party response slogan

- "It's a chicken and egg situation - Which came first?"

About the Author

Cradle fed crawfish, gumbo and Saints football, Bronwyn came to age on Bourbon Street, where the beats of different drummers became the soundtrack of her life. After graduating from Louisiana State University, Bronwyn packed a bottle of Tabasco sauce in a bag, and headed out into the world - first to Botswana as a wide-eyed idealistic Peace Corps Volunteer, then to Dallas, Texas as a naive federal employee, before landing in the middle of the South Pacific in American Samoa as the great protector of mangroves. When she was voted off the island, fate led her to Maryland, where she now lives today with her family.

Bronwyn's writing is pulled from her experiences traveling, living abroad and her penchant for finding or rather placing herself in unique situations - good and bad - which serve as fertile ground for good stories like playing professional football, losing the first female boxing match in American Samoa, being the second to last finisher in the Dublin marathon, making it 3/4 of the way up Kilimanjaro, buying a yacht with no boating experience, coconut crab hunter, driving an 18-wheeler, pulling metal out of dumpsters to sell, participating in medical research, professional eulogist, substitute teaching, fake patient for nursing students, industry taste tester, mystery shopper, beekeeper, preacher, foster parent, adoptive parent, PTA treasurer, church lady, voice over actor, magician and for the purposes of this book, backyard chicken farmer.

Acknowledgements

No woman is an island - neither is a book. Thank you to all who have helped to hatch Roost. The great folks at Apprentice House Publishing for working harder than a hen hauling wood. My dad - whose edits ensured that the book was safe for my mother to read. My mom, for teaching me how to play with words. Vikki and Kristi for their hawk-eyed editing skills. Coreen - my backyard chicken mentor. The amazing online community of backyard chicken farmers - who always seemed to have the answers to my chicken questions. The namesakes - Nicole, Glynn Ann, Todd and Ellen - who put up with having chickens named after them. My partner in life and all things chickens, Christina. The boys, Mason and Dylan, second generation backyard chicken farmers. And most importantly, the chickens, Nicole, Glynn Ann, Todd and Ellen, who gave their lives so that this book could live.

Apprentice
House Press
Loyola University Maryland

Apprentice House is the country's only campus-based, student-staffed book publishing company. Directed by professors and industry professionals, it is a nonprofit activity of the Communication Department at Loyola University Maryland.

Using state-of-the-art technology and an experiential learning model of education, Apprentice House publishes books in untraditional ways. This dual responsibility as publishers and educators creates an unprecedented collaborative environment among faculty and students, while teaching tomorrow's editors, designers, and marketers.

Outside of class, progress on book projects is carried forth by the AH Book Publishing Club, a co-curricular campus organization supported by Loyola University Maryland's Office of Student Activities.

Eclectic and provocative, Apprentice House titles intend to entertain as well as spark dialogue on a variety of topics. Financial contributions to sustain the press's work are welcomed. Contributions are tax deductible to the fullest extent allowed by the IRS.

To learn more about Apprentice House books or to obtain submission guidelines, please visit www.apprenticehouse.com.

Apprentice House
Communication Department
Loyola University Maryland
4501 N. Charles Street
Baltimore, MD 21210
Ph: 410-617-5265 • Fax: 410-617-2198
info@apprenticehouse.com • www.apprenticehouse.com

CPSIA information can be obtained
at www.ICGtesting.com
Printed in the USA
LVHW05s0151191018
594106LV00009B/278/P

9 781627 201834